THE
CHRISTMAS
ALMANAC

Michael Stephenson

Oxford University Press

396.268282

Oxford University Press, Walton Street, Oxford OX2 6DP
Oxford New York Toronto
Delhi Bombay Calcutta Madras Karachi Petaling Jaya Singapore Hong Kong Tokyo Nairobi
Dar es Salaam Cape Town Melbourne Auckland
and associated companies in
Berlin Ibadan

Oxford is a trade mark of Oxford University Press

A CIP catalogue record for this book is available from the British Library
ISBN 0 19 278132 4

This book was designed and produced by Mirabel Books Limited, PO Box 1214, London SW6 7ES

Jacket design by Glynn Pickerill
Front cover illustration by Robin Lawrie
Back cover illustration by Richard Hook
Edited by John Gilbert
Composition by Flying Dutchman Production Studio

Printed and bound in Belgium by Proost International Book Production, Turnhout

CONTENTS

PHOTO AND ILLUSTRATION CREDITS

Le carnaval à différentes époques.
Les Saturnales chez les anciens Romains. Avant-coureurs des fêtes du carnaval.

1

THE WINTER SOLSTICE

The meaning of Christmas

Christmas is the special religious ceremony in the Christian church that celebrates the birth of Jesus Christ. Christmas comes from two Old English words, '*Cristes*' and '*maesse*', meaning 'Christ's mass'. The word '*maesse*', in turn, is derived from the Latin *missa*, which means either 'sending away' (as on a mission) or 'bringing together'. It also means 'bread'.

Christmas is celebrated in midwinter. Yet hundreds, even thousands, of years before the birth of Christ, people of many countries held celebrations, partly religious and partly festive, around the end of December. And what is particularly interesting about these ritual ceremonies is that they are similar, in many ways, to those of Christmas itself. The echoes of such early celebrations, linking us to our ancient ancestors, bring an added excitement to our own Christmas.

The long dark night of winter

The peoples of the ancient world, originally hunter-gatherers and later farmers, were completely dependent on the great cycles of nature, the changing seasons: spring and summer, bringing warmth and plenty, autumn and winter, threatening cold and scarcity. It was hardly surprising, then, that many of them worshipped the sun, the glowing symbol of life

and hope. Without the sun, crops could not grow nor could living things flourish. Winter was the dark season when the earth seemed to be locked in the icy grip of black and evil forces. The long dark nights were full of terrors, alive with ghosts, goblins, and wicked spirits waiting to seize the weak and sick and drag them down into the underworld.

During the cold months of winter, food was scarce, wild animals roamed the woods and mountains, and death was common. Indeed, at this time of year, the 'winter solstice', when the northern part of the earth is furthest from the sun, many people believed that the sun itself had died. They feared that it would never return and that they would starve. With good reason was winter regarded as the season of death.

Our Christmas meal echoes the early Christian mass, meaning a time of being together.

◁ The Saturnalia festivities of the Ancient Romans took place in December and could, to put it mildly, be unruly affairs.

A medieval calendar showing the characteristic tasks for each month of the year.

Bonfires and sacrifices

In order to scare away the spirits of the night and to encourage the sun's return, people would often light bonfires at the time of the winter solstice. Sometimes they would make sacrifices to the sun god, usually of animals, but occasionally of humans. In the far north of Europe, for example, some tribes held ceremonies in which they killed wild boar and horses. The Druids were known to make human sacrifices to their fertil-

The rising sun (from a medieval coat of arms) was a symbol not only of the victory of spring over winter, but also of Jesus Christ.

ity gods. The victims were usually criminals or prisoners taken in battle. Customs of this kind continued in some parts of the world even after Christianity arrived. Many centuries later, the Aztecs of Central America made human sacrifices to appease their sun god.

After 22 December, the days gradually become longer, the ice melts, the sun reappears and warm spring rains herald new crop growth. People could once again look forward to the rebirth of nature. There would be food for themselves and their animals. Newborn babies would stand a better chance of survival.

Rejoicing in the thought that the worst part of the year was over, celebrating the passage from darkness to light, people would accompany their religious rites with eating, drinking, and merrymaking. Of all the traditions of Christmas, it is perhaps this spirit of festivity that most closely links us at this season with our distant ancestors.

Saturnalia in ancient Rome

Paper hats from Christmas crackers, coins in Christmas puddings, Christmas candles and decorations, presents on Boxing Day, pantomime horses—all these familiar traditions may have their origins in festivities that date back more than two thousand years.

Every winter, on 17 December, the people of ancient Rome began a wild party that lasted seven days. The festival, called Saturnalia, was in honour of Saturn, the god of agriculture, from whose name we get Saturday. The winter solstice meant that spring was not far away, and so the god of all growing things had to be honoured. There were noisy processions through the streets, candles were lit to symbolize the rebirth of the year, houses were decorated with laurel and other greenery—just as we use holly and ivy today—and presents were exchanged.

During this week of celebration, life was turned upside down. The rulers were governed by the ruled. The rich fed the poor. Masters wore the *pilleus*, the cap normally reserved for slaves, and gave them gifts—an origin, possibly, of the English Boxing Day, when masters gave money and other presents to their servants and apprentices. The courts of justice were closed and no one could be convicted of a crime.

The Lords of Misrule

According to one ancient Roman observer, 'Men dressed as women or masqueraded in the hides of animals'. There may be links here, perhaps, with the modern pantomime custom of men taking the role of women (Widow Twankey), women playing men (Principal Boy, Peter Pan, etc) and actors dressing up as the front and hind parts of a comical horse.

The modern habit of placing a coin or trinket in the Christmas pudding is very similar to the Saturnalia custom of hiding a dried bean in the food. The person who found it, even if he were a slave, was elected master of the revels, a king for the holidays with special privileges.

The traditions of the Roman Saturnalia found their way to all parts of the Empire, blending with customs that already existed and influencing the way in which people celebrated the end of the year.

The clowning of Saturnalia was common in medieval Christmas celebrations. In some of the larger houses a master of ceremonies was chosen who had the power to make anyone, high or low born, do as he, the Lord of Misrule, wished. In a Europe controlled by the Church and the nobility, Christmas was a time to let off steam and have some fun. In France, the Feast of the Ass permitted ordinary people to poke fun at the Church. An ass was dressed up in priest's clothes and led into church where comic versions of the service were held.

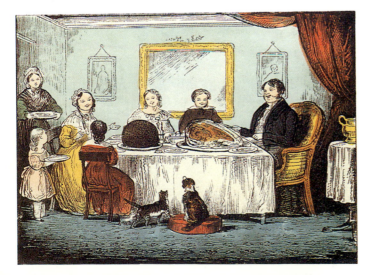

The tradition of hiding a coin in the Christmas pudding goes back at least to the time of the ancient Roman festival of Saturnalia, when a bean was hidden in a cake.

In England, the period from St Nicholas' Day (6 December) to Holy Innocents' Day (28 December) was a further reminder of Saturnalia. A choirboy was chosen to be bishop, dressed in his robes and allowed to hold services. Meanwhile the lad's masters had to obey his wishes and give him gifts. During the reign of Henry VIII, the tradition died out, although it was revived under Mary I until it was finally abolished by Elizabeth I.

Mithras: god of the undefeated sun

The cult of the god Mithras, known as the 'bull-slayer' and often represented as sacrificing a bull, was a form of sun worship that began in Persia (known today as Iran) at least 200 years before Christ, and then spread through the countries of the Mediterranean. Mithraism became very popular in the Roman Empire, especially in the army. In the first century AD, as the legions marched into Israel (the land of Christ's birth), Britain, Germany, and Gaul, today called France, they took Mithras with them. His birthday, known in Latin as *Natalis Sol Invictus*—the birthday of the Unconquered Sun—was a time of great rejoicing. Mithras had such a powerful following that the early Christian Church feared it might even threaten the survival of their still young religion. Indeed, some Christians used the popular festival of Mithras' birth for their own purpose of celebrating the birth of Jesus.

Like Jesus, Mithras was said to have been born on 25 December of a virgin mother, in a cave something like the dark animal shed in Bethlehem. Like Christ, too, he had twelve companions. Similarly, Mithras died at Easter time, was buried and rose again. In ancient art he was often shown as a lamb, as was Jesus. His name also meant 'deliverer' and 'bearer of light'.

Mithras was not the only ancient god to bear some resemblance to Christ. The Greek god Apollo, the Babylonian god Baal, and the Egyptian gods Osiris and Horus (born on 26 and 27 December respectively) were likewise associated with sun worship. The Indian god Krishna was also born in a cave, with a star shining above. An attempt was made to kill Krishna in infancy and a massacre of small children was ordered, just like that carried out by Herod during Christ's childhood.

Sun worshippers of the North

The sun was worshipped in many parts of northern Europe where winters were particularly cold and dark. Centuries before the birth of Christ, Germanic and Celtic tribes would gather around huge bonfires in the deepest part of winter, not just to keep warm but also to ward off the evil spirits believed to be lurking in the surrounding darkness.

Some of the ways by which the pagan Norsemen marked the winter solstice have echoed down the centuries and influenced the way we celebrate our modern Christmases. We know the Norsemen better as Vikings, sea-going warriors who raided England, Scotland, Ireland, and other parts of Europe from about AD 800 and for over 200 years after. But, in fact, Norse beliefs and legends go back to a much earlier period. The Norsemen worshipped the sun and saw it as a great wheel which, as it turned, changed the seasons. Their word for wheel was 'houl' or 'hioul', and this may be the origin of the word 'yule'.

As they sat around the bonfire, they told stories of men transformed into werewolves or of demon women called Valkyries who searched for souls to take to Valhalla, the realm of the dead. From goblets made of animal horn, Norse tribesmen drank a powerful brew of mead—a kind of ale sweetened with honey and flavoured with herbs.

The winter festival also honoured the powerful Norse god of war, Thor, from whom we get the word Thursday. Thor was particularly associated with thunder. And as we shall see, another of our connections between past and present involves thunder and mistletoe.

The Druids

The earliest religions believed that everything in the natural world was divine. Gods lived in the sun and moon, in wind and water, in thunder and lightning, in rocks and, particularly, in trees. For the Druids, a priestly Celtic tribe that lived in Britain, Ireland, and

A werewolf attacks a traveller (by Hans Weiditz, 1517). The deepest months of winter were considered a time when the forces of darkness and evil were particularly active.

The mistletoe bears its fruit during the winter—a symbol of life during the dead season.

the sacred oak. The procession was led by the tribal poets known as the bards, followed by a herald and then—the most important person of all—the Arch Druid. He wore flowing white robes, gold bands or bracelets on his arms, and a golden chain around his neck.

The Arch Druid would climb the oak until he reached the lowest branch on which mistletoe grew. Then, with a ceremonial sickle or knife, he would cut the sacred plant and carefully gather it into the folds of his gown, taking care not to let it touch the ground. The mistletoe was then broken up into many pieces and handed around among the worshippers, who were also blessed by the Arch Druid.

Health and love

The Druids also called mistletoe *omnia sanitatem*, meaning 'that which heals all', and used it as a medicine. It was believed even to heal hearts, so that if, for example, two enemies met under a tree bearing mistletoe, they were not allowed to fight. Mistletoe in the home had the same meaning. Anyone entering a home decorated with sprigs of the plant was entitled to receive shelter and protection. Some say it was even part of the Druid wedding ceremony.

In Scandinavia (the region in northern Europe roughly equivalent to modern Sweden, Norway, Denmark, and Finland), mistletoe has long been associated with Freyja, the goddess of love. But the early Christian Church wanted nothing to do with

Gaul, the oak was the sacred centre-point of their worship. The Druids were a mysterious group concerning whom nothing was recorded until Julius Caesar wrote about them after his conquest of Gaul in 58–51 BC. The Druid cult had virtually ended by AD 500, by which time Christianity had taken its place. The word 'druid' means 'knowing the oak tree'. The oak is, moreover, one of the trees on which the mistletoe plant grows, and thus mistletoe, too, was sacred to the Druids.

The word 'mistletoe' comes from the Old English *mistletan*, meaning 'different or special twig'. The ancient Greeks called it *phoradendron* or 'tree thief', a plant that lives off another tree as a kind of parasite. It favours the oak, although it can live on other trees as well. Mistletoe is a yellow-green plant with waxy white berries. Because it bore its fruit in winter, the ancient Greeks and Romans, and, particularly, the Druids, also associated it with fertility.

Oak trees tend frequently to be struck by lightning. For the Druids, thunder and lightning were considered to be direct signs from the gods, and this close association of the oak with the deadly power of the heavens would certainly have inspired feelings of special awe and reverence.

The mistletoe ceremony

The Druids held one of their biggest festivals during the winter solstice at the end of December. Men, women, and children trooped into the forest to greet

Who put the 'X' in Xmas?

is the first letter of the Greek word for Christ—*Xristos*—and for the early Christians, most of whom spoke and wrote Greek, the word signified 'Christ's Mass'. As the centuries passed, however, fewer and fewer people understood ancient Greek. They thought the 'X' had some pagan meaning and that the word 'Xmas' showed disrespect. Even today some people do not like the abbreviation.

The yule log represents the light that shines and warms in the darkness and cold of winter. It is also the hope of the light and warmth of the spring to come.

pagan kissing. Mistletoe was banned, and even today some churches refuse to include it in their Christmas decoration.

The yule log

The Celts believed that the sun stood still for twelve days during the winter solstice. Our twelve days of Christmas may have started with this belief. The Druids, for example, would bless a log, the yule log, and keep it burning for twelve days. Allowing the log to go out might bring great misfortune to the community. The power of light would have been conquered by darkness. And keeping a small piece to light the yule log next winter would ensure that good luck was carried on from year to year.

From the time of the Druids right through until the last century, the tradition lived on and it was still considered important to keep the log alight either for twelve hours of the day or for the whole twelve days of Christmas. The idea lingered that evil spirits could enter the house if the flame were to go out. And as in those olden times, a piece of the yule log was usually kept for the following year's celebrations. In Germany, for example, the ash and charcoal of the *Christbrand* or *Christholz* were kept in the home all year round to protect it from lightning—a direct link with the pagan past.

The seventeenth-century English poet Robert Herrick wrote:

> Kindle the Christmas brand, and then
> 'Till sunset let it burn
> Which quenched, then lay it up again,
> 'Till Christmas next return.
>
> Part must be kept, wherewith to tend
> The Christmas log next year;
> And if 'tis safely kept, the Fiend
> Can do no mischief here.

Choosing the log

The yule log—as big as would fit into the hearth—was cut in the woods on Christmas Eve. It was essential for it to be chopped down freshly rather than bought, otherwise it would lose its power. Even stealing one was considered better than buying one.

Ash was often the wood of first choice. Ash burns well and is quite easy to find in northern Europe. For Christians it has always had a special meaning, too, as it was thought by some to be the wood from which Christ's cross was made.

In southern France the yule log, known as the *tréfoire*, was ceremoniously dragged home by the whole family. Wine was thrown over it, usually by the youngest child. The log was then paraded around the kitchen three times before being laid in the hearth and lit.

In Yugoslavia a young tree was felled a day or two before Christmas Eve and sawn into logs which were then decorated with flowers. On Christmas Eve the family threw corn and wine over the log and on Christmas Day they scattered wheat on it, saying together, 'Christ is born'. In England, too, the log was often sprinkled with cider or ale, and corn.

There was a belief in Scandinavia that the yule log warmed the ghosts of the family dead who returned to their home at Christmas. Even today some Scandinavian families set an extra place at table for the spirit of a returning ancestor.

In Scandinavia it is traditional to leave a place at the Christmas table for the ghosts of the family's ancestors. The yule log was thought to warm the spirits from the chilly netherworld.

In many northern European countries it was also traditional to light a special Christmas candle. This yule candle, usually made of red wax and about 18 inches long, was lit on Christmas Eve along with the yule log. Similarly, it was regarded as very unlucky if the candle went out during the twelve days of Christmas.

Hanukkah: the Jewish winter solstice

Like Christmas, the Jewish festival of Hanukkah falls during the darkest days of December, and it, too, is a time for fun and gifts. The Hanukkah holidays fall on different days in December each year. Like the Christian Easter, for example, it is a 'movable feast'. It is also a celebration of light, as symbolized by the candles of the eight-branched *menorah*.

Some 200 years before the birth of Christ, the Jewish people lived in Judaea, a part of Palestine then ruled by the Greek-born King of Syria, Antiochus IV. When the king plundered the treasures of the holiest Jewish shrine, the Temple in Jerusalem, the Jews rebelled. The uprising was led first by the elderly priest Mattathias and then—more successfully—by Judah the Maccabee, which some translate as 'Judah the Hammerer'.

After years of armed struggle, Jerusalem was captured by the Maccabees but the Temple had been almost destroyed by Antiochus' soldiers. The Jews cleaned the Temple but when the time came for its ceremonial reopening, there was not enough sacred oil left to relight the candlestick. Judah found only one jar of oil, just sufficient to keep the candles lit for eight days.

The feast of lights

Nowadays the holiday of Hanukkah is celebrated for eight days in memory of the Maccabeean uprising and the Temple miracle. Eight candles are lit on the *menorah* with a special ninth candle called the *shammas*, or 'servant' light—the one light able to kindle many. On the first night one candle is lit, on the second night two, and so on throughout the eight days. After the lighting of the candles, everyone joins

During each evening of the Jewish Hanukkah festivities a candle on the *menorah* is lit.

in the singing of a hymn that commemorates the deeds of the Maccabees. The *menorah* is displayed in a window or doorway to proclaim the coming of the light.

One of the games children play at Hanukkah is spinning a four-sided top called the *dreidel*, each face of which bears a Hebrew letter. This game of chance is won by the player whose side lands uppermost when the top has finished spinning.

Hanukkah is a great time for giving presents but not so much for sending cards, which happens more during the New Year celebrations of Rosh Hashanah, a holiday that falls on different days each year at the end of September or the beginning of October (see page 113). A traditional gift is 'Hanukkah gelt', or little chocolate coins covered with gold foil.

The traditional hymn sung at Hanukkah, to celebrate the rededication of the Temple, is *Ma'oz t'sur* ('Rock of Ages').

2

THE FIRST CHRISTMAS

The Roman world of Jesus

The world into which Jesus was born was ruled from Rome and had been part of the all-powerful Roman Empire for more than sixty years. The land of Palestine, as it was called by the Romans, had been settled by the Israelite or Jewish tribes about twelve centuries earlier, and the pages of the Old Testament describe the events that involved the Jewish people and their neighbours over the next 700 or so years. During this time, Israel came under the rule of the Assyrians, the Babylonians, the Persians, the Greeks, and the Syrians. Pompey the Great established Syria as a Roman province, captured Jerusalem in 63 BC, and extended Roman rule from Syria to the whole of Israel. At that time the country was broadly divided into the regions of Galilee, Judaea, Samaria, and Idumaea. It was in Judaea, with its capital of Jerusalem, that most of the Jewish population lived.

The Emperor Augustus

At the time Jesus was born, the Roman Emperor Augustus was probably the most powerful man in the world. As ruler of the Roman Empire he controlled most of southern Europe and the Mediterranean. Born in Rome in the very year Pompey had captured Jerusalem, Caius Julius Caesar Octavianus, a name commonly shortened to Octavian, was the great-nephew, and later the adopted son and heir, of

The Emperor Augustus, during whose rule Jesus was born.

≺ A lamp from the time of the Roman Emperor Augustus.

the famous Julius Caesar. When Caesar was murdered in 44 BC, the nineteen-year-old Octavian set out on his climb to power.

Octavian's great rival in Rome was Marcus Antonius (Mark Antony), but after Octavian's fleet won a victory over Antony at the sea battle of Actium in 31 BC, Octavian became 'master of all'. The Romans made him their emperor, to be known as Caesar Augustus, and when he died in AD 14 they declared him a god. He was succeeded by Tiberius, in whose reign Jesus would be crucified.

Puppet rulers

The Romans used local governors or kings to run the country for them. These 'puppet-rulers' were expected to keep everything in order, to put down any revolts and, above all, to make sure the people were taxed. The money from these taxes was needed to pay for the lavish way of life in Rome. There were also the hundreds of garrisons and tens of thousands of soldiers who had to be paid to keep the Roman Empire under control.

In 37 BC, Octavian appointed a man named Herod to be king of Judaea. Herod was not a Jew, for his family were Idumaean—Arabs from the western shore of the Dead Sea. His father had helped Julius Caesar when he was trying to conquer Egypt, and had been rewarded with Roman citizenship. Herod himself was later made military governor of Galilee and then, at the age of thirty-six, king of Judaea, although he had to answer to the Roman masters in Syria.

An extremely cruel man but also a clever politician, Herod was by now very rich, having received half the proceeds of all the copper mined in Cyprus and having made huge profits out of taxing the people of Palestine. He used some of this money to build a great city by the sea called Caesarea, named after Caesar Augustus, and to rebuild the Temple in Jerusalem.

Herod's bloodthirsty reign

'He was no king but the most cruel tyrant who ever ascended the throne. He murdered a vast number of people and the lot of those he left behind was so miserable that the dead might count themselves fortunate. He not only tortured his subjects singly but ill-treated whole

The baby Jesus in the animal stall in which he was born. The manger, or animal feeding box, which served as his crib, is behind his mother, Mary.

communities. In order to beautify foreign cities he robbed his own, and made gifts to foreign nations which were paid for with Jewish blood . . . Within a few years the Jews suffered more misery through Herod than their forefathers had done.'

This was written by the Jewish historian Flavius Josephus just a few years after Herod's death.

Josephus had good grounds for his accusation. The first ten years of Herod's reign was a bloodbath. He wiped out the old royal family and the nobility. He murdered his wife Mariamne, his sons Alexander, Aristobulos, and Antipater, as well as his mother-in-law, brother-in-law, and the husbands of his sister Salome. Anyone who opposed him, or whom he even suspected of opposing him, was killed.

The Gospel story

The birth of Christ is mentioned only in two of the four Gospels, those of Matthew and Luke. Mark and John both start their stories with John the Baptist and Jesus' baptism. Like many people in the early Christian Church, they were not interested in the details of Christ's birth, considering his teaching and the events surrounding his death to be much more important.

Scholars think that Mark's Gospel was probably the first to be written, perhaps only forty years after Christ's death. Matthew and Luke wrote their Gospels about sixty or seventy years after the Crucifixion. Matthew was one of the twelve disciples (friends of Jesus chosen by Jesus himself). Although Matthew had a close connection to Jesus, he was not, of course, present at Jesus' birth. Luke almost certainly did not know Jesus personally, and had to research his story using other sources.

Matthew says nothing of the angel who announces to Mary that she will have a child. He makes no mention of the Roman tax that caused the Holy Family to travel to Bethlehem, of Caesar Augustus who

A fourteenth-century Italian painting that shows Mary presenting Jesus to the elders of the Temple at Jerusalem.

ordered it, or of Cyrenius, then the governor of Syria. There is no reference to the stable, the manger, the ox, or the ass. Matthew says simply that the Wise Men entered a 'house' to see the infant. He does not mention the visit Mary made to her cousin Elizabeth or that Elizabeth gave birth to John the Baptist a few months before Jesus was born. Nor does he state, as does Luke, that Jesus was circumcized on the eighth day after his birth, like all Jewish boy babies, and that he then was taken to the Temple at Jerusalem to be presented to the Lord.

Luke does not mention the Wise Men or the Star of Bethlehem. He tells us only that the shepherds came to glorify the Lord. Unlike Matthew, he omits the accounts of the Flight into Egypt and Herod's Massacre of the Innocents.

What neither Gospel mentions is the exact date of Christ's birth. All we have are clues.

When was Jesus born?

Five hundred and thirty years after Christ, a monk named Dionysius Exiguus (Denis the Small), who was a mathematician and astronomer living in Rome, was given the job of reforming the calendar and of fixing the exact year of Jesus' birth. He calculated that Jesus had been born in year 1 and stated that this was the date from which Christian history should be counted. There was only one problem. It is now clear that Dionysius had made a miscalculation of about four years. Although no one knows the precise year, experts are agreed that Jesus was born before the year 1.

'Magi', or astrologers, were important in the world into which Jesus was born. By studying the movements of the stars and planets, magi were believed to be able to predict events on Earth.

The census clues

Both Matthew and Luke say that Jesus was born while Herod was king of Judaea. Herod reigned from 37 BC to 4 BC.

Luke states that Caesar Augustus issued a decree that every subject of Roman rule throughout the Empire should be counted (by means of a census) in order to be taxed, and that this happened when Cyrenius was governor of Syria. The Jewish historian Josephus, writing very close to the time of Christ, says there was a census in AD 6–7, when Cyrenius was still governor. There is evidence that Cyrenius had been in the Holy Land and held a census in 8 BC, and it is probably this census that is mentioned in the Gospels. Tertullian, a Christian Roman lawyer who wrote about 200 years after Christ, states that Jesus was born in 7 or 8 BC.

The season and day

If it has been difficult to determine the year when Jesus was born, deciding the season, let alone the exact day, has posed even greater problems. Some scholars doubt whether the birth took place in winter and say this may simply be a link with pagan festivals at the end of December. They suggest it must have been in the spring, because Luke's Gospel mentions the shepherds guarding their flocks at night. They would only have taken such extra care during the

The shepherds about to be visited by an angel of the Lord to announce Christ's birth.

The Three Wise Men see the startling brightness of the star leading them to Bethlehem. Was it a comet, a supernova or a 'conjunction' of planets?

spring lambing season when prowling wolves or even lions might attack the flocks.

Nowhere in the Gospels or elsewhere in the Bible is the day of Jesus' birth given. Indeed, in the following 300 years or so, the early Christians did not celebrate his birth 'as if he were a Pharaoh'. It was his death that was important to them. Many of these Christians, for example, lived in Egypt, and they accepted the correct date as 6 January. Western Christians (mainly those living in Rome) rejected this date because they saw a great advantage in connecting the birth of Jesus with the old pagan festivals of Mithras and Saturnalia. It was a form of Christian take-over!

Christianity became an accepted religion of the Roman Empire in AD 312. Within another fifty or so years most Christian churches had recognized 25 December. Even today there are different Christmas Days within Christian churches. The Armenian Apostolic Church celebrates it on 6 January, while the Russian Orthodox Church has its Christmas Day on 7 January.

The Star of Bethlehem

Since biblical times, further clues have come from astronomers, who make a study of heavenly bodies, and from astrologers, who consider the influence of these heavenly bodies on human affairs.

On 17 December 1603 the Imperial Mathematician and Astronomer Royal to the Holy Roman Empire, Johannes Kepler, observed the 'conjunction' or 'coming together' of the planets Saturn and Jupiter. Of course, these planets did not literally come together, for they are many millions of miles apart. Looking from the Earth, however, the light from the planets appeared to merge into one very bright star. As Kepler watched the amazing occurrence from his observatory in Prague, he realized that what he was seeing might well have happened before, close to another Christmas more than 1600 years earlier. Perhaps this was what the Wise Men had seen? He began to do some calculations.

Kepler's theory

In astronomy it is possible to make fairly precise estimates of the past, as well as accurate predictions of the future. Kepler's astronomical tables showed clearly that a conjunction of Saturn and Jupiter had taken place in 6 BC.

To add weight to Kepler's explanation of the Star of Bethlehem, modern scholars have translated the writings of the ancient Babylonian School of Astrology at Sippar, which was active at the time of Jesus' birth. These writings confirm that a great conjunction took place in 7 BC, almost the same date as Kepler had calculated.

As the science of astronomy progressed, more accurate calculations could be made of what will happen to our solar system as well as what probably occurred at the time of Jesus' birth.

Jewish astrologers

Modern astronomy gives us even more details of this planetary conjunction. It appeared four times within ten months, first on 29 May 7 BC, then on 3 October and 4 December of the same year, and finally at the end of January of the next year, 6 BC.

Many Jewish astrologers went to study at the Sippar School of Astrology. Perhaps, on the roof of the school, some *magi*—men skilled in predicting celestial signs—witnessed the first conjunction in May. Ancient tradition said that the coming of the Messiah, or Saviour of the Jewish people, would be announced by just such an event. The Bible mentions 'wise men' from the East. This might well be a reference to astrologers travelling from Babylon. Moreover, they would probably have started out in October after the fierce heat of summer had died down, when their journey would be that much more comfortable.

Another clue to support Kepler's theory is that Jupiter and Saturn had special importance for ancient Jewish astrologers. Saturn was the planet which protected Israel, while Jupiter was associated with the coming of the Messiah. A conjunction of these two planets would have been doubly significant.

A supernova?

Some people do not agree with Kepler. For example, science fiction writer Arthur C. Clarke, the author of *2001*, believes there was an even closer conjunction of planets in 66 BC which, if you believe Kepler, 'should have brought a delegation of wise men to Bethlehem fifty-nine years too soon'.

Clarke's own theory is that only an exploding star or 'supernova' could have accounted for a light bright enough to have impressed people at the time so much that they would have noted it down. However, there are only two references to phenomena that could have been supernovas, in 134 BC and in AD 173. But something as incredibly bright as a comet or new supernova would surely have been noted by many people across the ancient world, and there is no mention of such appearances on either occasion.

Mary and Joseph

In Hebrew Mary's name was Miriam. Both she and her husband, Joseph, belonged to the 'house' or tribe

A medieval woodcut shows magi or astrologers sighting the image of Jesus in the star they are following to Bethlehem.

of David. We know that Jesus was her first child, but he may not have been her last. Mark's Gospel says that Jesus was 'the brother of James and Joses, and of Juda and Simon. And are not his sisters here with us?' Did Mary and Joseph have other children after Jesus

The naming of Jesus

The name 'Jesus' is the Greek version of the Hebrew name 'Joshua' or 'Jeshua', meaning 'a saviour'. 'Christ', again the Greek translation of the Hebrew 'Messiah', means 'the anointed' or 'the chosen one'. To anoint someone was to pour oil over their head as a sign that such a person was especially chosen by God. Sometimes Jesus is referred to as 'Emmanuel' or 'Immanuel', Hebrew for 'God with us'.

Jesus is known by a Greek name because the world he lived in was greatly influenced by the Greeks, even though by that time it was controlled by the Romans. Many of the grand buildings in Palestine were in the Greek style. Most people could read and speak Greek. And the Gospels were probably written in Greek.

A Jewish wedding feast in a wealthy household. This is the Marriage of Cana,
at which Jesus turned water into wine.

was born? Or were they the children of an earlier marriage of Joseph's? We simply do not know.

Joseph appears in the Bible mainly as part of the Nativity story. He is not mentioned at all in the Gospel according to Mark and only very briefly in John's Gospel.

In Jewish society, young men were normally expected to learn a manual trade or craft, even if they were going to become priests, doctors or lawyers. Joseph became a carpenter, as would his son, Jesus. This would have entailed more than woodwork and joinery. In those days carpenters took on small building jobs, and would be likely to know something about masonry and general building principles as well.

St Matthew goes to great lengths in his Gospel to trace Joseph's ancestry through forty-two generations—all the way back, through King David, to Abraham, the 'father' of the Jewish people. Luke, too, mentions that Joseph is part of this great family. Both writers wanted to stress that Jesus belonged to the family that had saved Israel in the past. The Messiah from the house of David—Jesus—would save Israel again in the future, just as the Old Testament prophets had predicted.

Joseph fades from the Gospel story after taking the twelve-year-old Jesus to the Temple at Jerusalem for Passover. Some people think that Joseph was much older than his wife Mary and that he probably died during Jesus' early teenage years.

Marriage in biblical times

Most Jewish marriages at the time of Mary and Joseph were arranged by the fathers of the bride and groom. Although it was important that the two people respected each other, they were not necessarily expected to be in love. Some cultures today, such as the Hindus, still favour arranged marriages.

Bethlehem was an important place in Jewish history even before Jesus' birth there. It was at Bethlehem that the great King David was anointed by the prophet Samuel to lead the Jewish people.

Once a proposal of marriage was made, the two fathers discussed money. In those days it was felt that to lose a daughter in marriage was to lose a worker. The girl's father expected to be paid to make up for the loss. This payment, known as the *mohar*, might be made in money, in cattle and other goods, in land, or a combination of all of these. The amount depended on how important the girl's family was in the local community.

After the *mohar* was agreed, the young man gave presents to the bride's family. This signified that the couple were engaged or 'espoused', meaning promised in marriage. Although they did not yet live together, they were bound by strict legal contract. Until the time of their actual marriage the boy and the girl had to be faithful to each other. That is why Joseph was so shocked when he learned that Mary was going to have a baby. He was so ashamed that he planned to lock her away. Only when he was visited by the angel, who explained the extraordinary circumstances of Mary's pregnancy, did Joseph understand what had happened to Mary and forgive her.

Cyrenius the governor

The Roman governor in charge of Syria at the time of Jesus' birth was P. Sulpicius Quirinius, otherwise known as Cyrenius. Judaea was by now part of the great Roman-controlled province known as Syria. An able soldier, who had been spotted and promoted by Augustus, Cyrenius came from a humble family, and was just the type of ambitious yet capable administrator that the Romans valued.

The tax-collecting activities of Cyrenius and the superstitious reaction of Herod to the news of Jesus' birth were to play decisive roles in the events surrounding the Holy Family.

The tax-gatherers

'And it came to pass in those days, that there went out a decree from Caesar Augustus that all the world should be taxed. (And this taxing

was first made when Cyrenius was governor of Syria.) And all went to be taxed, every one into his own city.'

The Gospel according to St Luke.

It is interesting that the census or tax ordered by Caesar Augustus is referred to only in Luke's Gospel and not in Matthew. Yet we know that Matthew himself was a tax-collector or customs official and the omission from his account is surprising.

Taxation affected everyone. Taxes were payable at frontier customs posts and on the sale of goods (like the Value Added Tax now payable in Britain and the EEC countries or the sales tax in the United States). There were taxes on religious worship and on property. And every individual paid a head or 'poll' tax.

Each censor appointed by the local ruler had to draw up an accurate list of everyone in the area who was liable for tax. Men might be required to do military service and it was the censor's job to register them.

Local tax offices had to raise taxes for a number of purposes. Money was needed to run the province, to pay tribute to Rome, and to show the governor a nice profit. To ensure that taxes were paid, the governor could threaten to use force or punish offenders in other ways. It was obviously very important to be counted at the right time, and it was for this reason that Joseph was forced to take his pregnant wife on such a long and dangerous journey.

Mary and Joseph were obliged to go to the censor's office in Bethlehem because that was the town from which their families had originally come. Joseph's family may still have owned property in Bethlehem which would have had to be registered for tax.

The sacred town of Bethlehem

'But thou Bethlehem Ephratah, though thou be little among the thousands of Judah yet out of thee shall he come forth unto me that is to be ruler in Israel.'

Micah, 5:2.

There was another good reason why Mary and Joseph wanted Jesus to be born in Bethlehem. They knew that the prophets of the Old Testament had predicted that this town would be the birthplace of the Messiah.

Centuries before Jesus, another shepherd, the boy David, was looking after his flock outside Bethlehem. God directed the prophet Samuel to choose the boy to be the future leader of Israel.

Because of these associations, Bethlehem held a special place in Jewish history. It was the birthplace of saviours.

Nazareth

The town of Nazareth lies midway between the Sea of Galilee to the east and the Mediterranean in the west. In biblical times it was hardly famous, and is not even mentioned in the Old Testament. Indeed it was considered a bit of a joke. The people of Galilee were thought to be rough and uncivilized, and many who lived in Nazareth were cave-dwellers. In the Gospel according to St John, the story is told that

Travel in biblical times could be very dangerous. There were not only wild animals but also bands of robbers, like those who set about the man discovered here by the Good Samaritan.

when someone learned that Jesus came from Nazareth, he blurted out, 'Can there any good thing come out of Nazareth?'

Despite the town's reputation, this was exactly the right environment for Jesus. As St Luke makes clear, from his birth Jesus was to be the champion of the humble and the poor.

The road to Bethlehem

Even before the Romans took over Israel there was a good road system, although such roads were often no more than tracks. The best were hard-surfaced, either paved with stones or cut from rock. The worst were just dirt trails that covered travellers in dust during the summer and bogged them down in mud during the winter rains. The road from Nazareth in southern Galilee to Bethlehem in the south of Judaea was one of the country's main highways, marked out with kerb stones and repaired fairly regularly. But by our standards it would still have been narrow and quite dangerous.

The distance between Nazareth and Bethlehem is about 120 miles (190 kilometres). Mary and Joseph

Mary and Joseph arrive at the inn or 'khan'— a resting place for the caravans carrying goods across the country.

Mary and Joseph may well have travelled from Nazareth to Bethlehem as part of a merchant's convoy or caravan.

probably travelled by donkey, in which case they would have been lucky to cover 15 miles (25 kilometres) each day. Horses were certainly a good deal speedier and could cover about 25 miles (40 kilometres) a day, but they were only used by the Roman army and wealthy people.

Discomfort and danger

The journey would have been even slower and more uncomfortable than usual because Mary was about to have a baby and must have needed to stop and rest

Traditionally there are always three Wise Men,
but the Bible stories of Jesus' birth never say exactly
how many there were.

frequently. Few doctors would recommend a rocking, jolting ride on the back of a donkey for the health either of the mother-to-be or her unborn child. The journey may well have brought on the birth more quickly than anyone had expected; and perhaps the reason that Mary gave birth to her baby in a lowly stable was that there simply was not time to make more elaborate arrangements.

Mary and Joseph might have travelled in a large group or 'caravan' of camels. Many of those in the caravan would have been merchants taking their goods to cities such as Jerusalem. There was safety in numbers. Apart from the danger from wild animals, there were bands of robbers along the way waiting to pounce on single travellers or small groups that could not put up much defence. The traveller beaten up and robbed by bandits in the Gospel story of the Good Samaritan cannot have been an unusual or isolated incident.

No room at the inn

Bethlehem, which in Hebrew means 'house of bread', is 5 miles (8 kilometres) south of Jerusalem. It is quite high up—about 2500 feet (750 metres) above sea level—seated on the main ridge that runs from north to south down almost the whole length of the country that was then Palestine and is today Israel.

At the time of Jesus' birth Bethlehem was surrounded by pasture on which flocks of sheep and goats fed. There was probably more woodland around the town than there is now. As a result of over-grazing, the amount of desert has increased over the centuries and this area today is less green than it would have been when Jesus was born.

Because Bethlehem was on a main north-south trade route, many caravans of travellers would have passed through the town. The inn that sheltered these merchants was called a *khan*—a kind of motel for camels.

We feel shocked that Mary and Joseph had to stay overnight in a stable because the local inn was full. But it was not uncommon then for people to live alongside animals. In fact, it was normal in remote country areas and has remained so until the present day. The humans lived in a kind of loft while a variety of animals such as cows, chickens, and goats were accommodated below. In winter this arrangement certainly made for more warmth, even if rather smellier than most of us would like.

'Lying in a manger'

The 'manger' in which the baby Jesus was laid was the feeding rack for cows and horses. It was made of wood and shaped like an open basket. If it had been lined with straw and also perhaps a woollen blanket or a sheepskin it would have been very comfortable, in fact a perfect crib.

We do not know whether anyone helped Mary when she gave birth to Jesus. It was usual for women from the community to give advice and assistance during childbirth, and there would certainly have been such women in Bethlehem at the time. Custom, however, would not have allowed Joseph to be present.

As soon as the baby was born it was washed and rubbed with salt. This acted as an antiseptic and helped to prevent infection. Then the baby was wrapped quite tightly in bandages known as 'swaddling bands'. People in those days believed that unless the baby's legs were kept straight they might become weak or grow crooked. Even today, newborn babies are tightly wrapped in a blanket to make them feel warm and secure.

Each of the gifts given by the Magi had special significance: gold for kingship; frankincense for holiness; myrrh for anointing kings and priests.

The Wise Men

The 'Wise Men' are mentioned only in the Gospel of St Matthew and he does not actually state that there were three. The tradition started because people assumed that since he referred to three gifts—'gold and frankincense and myrrh'—they must have been given by three separate individuals.

Although St Matthew does not call them 'magi', tradition has always given the wise men that name. The word *magus* (*magi* is the plural) is related to the word 'magic' and, as we have seen, means someone who was skilled in astrology and the occult.

In the ancient world, all aspects of magic were taken very seriously. Magic was used to foretell the future, to chart a person's destiny according to heavenly signs, to decide the right time to make an important journey, or to initiate a new venture by consulting 'oracles'. In the Old Testament there are

many references to the movements of the stars as signs of God's power.

Because astrology was so important, it would have been fitting that the birth of the Messiah should be heralded by what appeared to be a magical positioning of the stars. The Gospel writers would have pointed this out to their readers in order to emphasize the significance of the event.

It is also important for another reason. Matthew reported that the wise men 'fell down and worshipped Him'. This implied that they were saying to Jesus, 'You are a greater power than all the old forces of our magic. We bow down and recognize it.' In other words, the old pagan religions were giving way to the new religion called Christianity.

The first gifts

Exchanging gifts was, and still is, a very important ritual in the Middle East. Even today it is considered an insult, when visiting a home, not to bring a gift, which must reflect the standing of the receiver.

Each of the three gifts given to the infant Jesus by the wise men had a special meaning.

The first was gold, which represented kingship. The second was frankincense, a sweet-smelling gum from a tree that grows in Arabia, burnt during religious ceremonies and therefore associated with holiness and prayer. The third was myrrh, also a gum from an Arabian tree, used as an oil for anointing priests and kings, but also for embalming the body after death. When myrrh was mixed with wine, it could act as a drug, dulling pain. Sometimes it was given to those about to be crucified in order to ease their suffering. Indeed, it may have been such a mixture that was offered to, and rejected by, Jesus during his crucifixion. So its association with death foretold Jesus' fate on the cross.

Angels always came to Joseph in dreams.

From magi to kings

In the Bible, the wise men were not referred to as kings. Not until the Middle Ages did the legend of the three kings become popular. One was said to be Melchior, King of Arabia, who at the age of sixty was the oldest of the three. His was the gift of gold. The second was Gaspar, sometimes called Caspar, the twenty-year-old King of Tarsus, who brought myrrh in a gold-mounted horn. The third, Balthasar, aged forty, was the dark-skinned King of Ethiopia, the land of spices. He gave Jesus frankincense in a special container called a censor.

It was said that Mary gave each of the kings a band from Jesus' swaddling clothes. All three were converted to Christianity and supposedly died for their faith in India. Legend has it that their bodies were sent to Constantinople (modern Istanbul in Turkey) by the Empress Helena, mother of Constantine the Great. The bodies were later moved to Milan and then transported by the German Emperor Barbarossa to

The three magi were usually represented as kings; Melchior of Arabia, Caspar of Tarsus, and Balthasar of Ethiopia.

In this medieval woodcut, an angel appears to the shepherds and tells them of the birth of Jesus.

Some of the earliest images of winged spirits come from ancient Egypt. This one is from an ancient Egyptian tapestry curtain.

Cologne Cathedral, where there is today a tomb containing the relics.

These relics were reputed to have magical powers. In the Middle Ages travellers adopted the kings as their patron saints. Today, in Czechoslavakia, their initials, C, M, B, are written over the doors of the house on 6 January, the Feast of Epiphany. 'Epiphany' means 'to show', and it was on this day that Jesus was shown to the world, represented by the Magi. And on this same day, in Spain, where it is believed that the Three Kings travelled through the country on their way to Bethlehem, children fill their shoes with straw and leave them on the windowsill for the kings' horses. The shoes are then filled with presents.

Angels

The word 'angel' comes from the Greek *angelos*, meaning 'a messenger from God'. In the Gospel stories of the birth of Jesus, angels play a very important part. They bring good news as well as warnings of danger.

In St Matthew's Gospel angels make three appearances, but only to Joseph, in his dreams. The first angel tells him to take Mary as his wife, for she is to give birth to the Son of God who shall be called Jesus. The second angel warns Joseph of King Herod's plan to kill the baby Jesus and tells him to escape to Egypt with his family. The third angel gives Joseph the good news that Herod has died and that it is now safe to return home.

Angels are a good deal busier in St Luke's Gospel. The first to appear visits Elizabeth, Mary's cousin, to tell her she is to have a baby, John, who will grow up to be the great preacher, John the Baptist. The next angel, and the only one named in the Gospel stories, is the archangel Gabriel, who announces to Mary that she will give birth to the Son of God. This great visit is called the 'Annunciation', a term obviously connected with the word 'announce'.

The last angel to appear frightens the shepherds tending their flocks at night because he is surrounded by a dazzling light. This 'angel of the Lord' tells the shepherds of Christ's birth and where the baby is to be found. He is then joined by a great crowd of fellow angels who sing 'Glory to God in the highest, and on Earth peace, good will toward men.'

Angels in history

The earliest known image of winged angels dates from the ancient Egyptians. The Greeks later showed divine beings, such as Hermes the messenger, also

The Ranks of Angels (see page 25). As Christianity ➤ developed, many complicated systems were put forward for ranking angels according to their importance and function.

with wings. In Old Testament times the Jewish people thought of God as a powerful king or ruler. Of course, a king would be expected to have servants, advisers, and messengers—in fact, the entire retinue of a royal court. Thus God's courtiers were angels. And just as a king would also be expected to have an army, so God's soldiers, too, were angels.

As Christianity grew, so did the theories about angels. Hundreds of types were identified and many Christian thinkers tried to put them into some sort of order, rather on the lines of officers, non-commissioned officers, and 'other ranks' in an army. Some early writers even calculated exactly how many angels existed. In the fourteenth century, for example, there were believed to be 301,655,722 Hebrew-speaking angels, no more nor less!

The Virgin Mary and Jesus attended by the archangels Michael and Gabriel.

The Christian religion is not alone in recognizing angels, for they exist, too, in Hinduism, Buddhism and, of course, Judaism.

The image of angels

The Jews are forbidden by holy law to make images of heavenly beings and so there are no Jewish pictures or statues of angels, although there are many powerfully written descriptions of them. When the Jewish Scriptures, the Old Testament, became part of Christian literature, Christian artists were free to paint, draw, and sculpt the angels described in its pages.

For example, the prophet Isaiah says, 'I saw the Lord sitting upon a throne, high and lifted up. . . . Above it stood the seraphim. Each one had six wings. With two he covered his face, and with two he covered his feet, and with two he did fly.'

The Book of Revelation, in the New Testament, describes how a mighty angel came down from Heaven, 'clothed with a cloud, and a rainbow upon his head, and his face like the sun, and his feet like pillars of fire. And he had in his hand a little book, and the book was open. And he set his right foot upon the land. And he cried with a loud voice like the roar of a lion.' We think of the word 'angelic' as meaning sweet and baby-faced, but sometimes angels could be quite terrifying to mere humans.

A seraph, one of the highest ranking angels. Seraphim guarded the gate of the Garden of Eden to prevent Adam and Eve returning after they had been expelled.

Angelic duties

From the Bible we can get a pretty good idea of what angels did. Angel choirs and orchestras had to provide continuous music around the throne of God. 'Guardian angels' kept people from harm. One of their main duties was to act as messengers between God and Man. Angels also had God's permission to punish the wicked. The cherubim, angels particularly close to God, stopped Adam and Eve returning to the Garden of Eden. And one of the special duties of the archangel Michael was to gather the souls of good people who had died and escort them to God. Once in Heaven, these good souls became like angels themselves. By contrast, it was also the job of the 'recording angel' to keep a note of all the wicked things people did during their lives on Earth.

The ranks of angels

Various Christian thinkers came up with different ways of ranking angels. St Ambrose, for example, invented a system that listed angels according to their closeness to God and thus their importance:

1. *Seraphim* are the highest order. They have three pairs of wings and, in the Middle Ages, were always associated with the colour red.

2. *Cherubim* are the keepers of the celestial records and the givers of knowledge. They had swords of fire which, at one time, they used to prevent Adam and Eve returning to the Garden of Eden. In the Middle Ages they were associated with the colour blue, which was the colour of wisdom. As time passed, they were transformed into winged babies which, in Italian, are called *putti*.

3. *Denominations* supervise angelic duties.

4. *Thrones* bring God's justice to Man.

5. *Principalities* are the protectors of religion.

6. *Potentates* stop demons attempting to overthrow the world.

7. *Virtues* have the special responsibility to work miracles on Earth.

8. *Archangels*, together with *angels*, are the guardians of humans and all physical things. Although they do not rank very high, archangels are known to us by name. In Christianity the four principal archangels are Raphael, the 'Divine Healer'; Uriel, the 'Bringer of God's Light to Man'; Michael, 'Leader of the Heavenly Army', and Gabriel, the 'Chief Ambassador of God to Man'.

In the bleak midwinter

The climate of the Holy Land has probably changed very little since the time of Jesus. The six months from May to September are hot and dry. There are often heavy rains during December, January, and February. The daytime winter temperature usually is not less than 50°F (10°C), and although snow is rare, temperatures can fall at night to near freezing on the high hills, such as those of Bethlehem. The shepherds 'keeping watch over their flock at night' would almost certainly have been sitting around a fire, while Mary and Joseph would have wrapped themselves in woollen cloaks and perhaps even sheep and goat skins to keep warm.

The shepherds

'While shepherds watched their flocks by night,
All seated on the ground . . .'

A fascinating question has long intrigued many people. Why were the shepherds tending their flocks out in the open during the freezing winter weather? The answer might not only give us a much better idea of life in the time of Jesus but also shed some light on the time of year Jesus was born.

Some experts say that shepherds in those days would only have been out with their sheep in spring, during the vital lambing season. If too many lambs were lost, either from bad weather or wild animals, everyone in the tightly knit community suffered. In the more remote parts of Palestine there were wild dogs, wolves, and even mountain lions. So it was especially important for shepherds to be out protecting their flocks, particularly the vulnerable lambs. They would have armed themselves with slings and

A thirteenth-century illustration of the Holy Family's flight into Egypt.

wooden clubs, and they would certainly have built a fire to frighten off the predatory animals and to keep warm.

Other experts argue that in winter, when it can get very cold indeed up in the highlands around Bethlehem, most flocks of sheep and goats would have been kept indoors in simple covered pens. On the other hand, there are those who point out that the particular breed of sheep found in biblical Palestine were, like those still seen in the region, hardy animals tough enough to withstand cold weather out in the open. Many experts now think that Jesus was probably not born at the end of December but more likely during the spring.

The life of the shepherd

Sheep and goats were very important to the people of Palestine. They provided milk, wool and meat. The shepherd, therefore, was an important person in the community. He had to be familiar with the lie of the land on which his flock grazed. He needed to know which caves he might be able to use for shelter, where to find springs of water, and where hidden dangers lurked.

In the Bible, the shepherd was seen as much more than a humble farm worker. Indeed, he had a special significance that stretched back to the earliest history of the Jews. The figure of the shepherd represented the leader who cared for his people, someone who would guide them through danger and go to endless

pains to make sure they were safe and protected. Jesus was often described as a shepherd. And Jesus' ancestor, King David, had been a shepherd before being chosen to lead the people of Israel.

The Massacre of the Innocents

Like most rulers of his time, Herod placed great faith in astrology, believing that the stars and movements of the planets influenced daily life and were signs that foretold the future. The king knew that his Jewish subjects expected a Messiah, the Saviour, to come to free them. When that happened, Herod realized he would be finished. He was convinced that certain signs in the night sky would foretell this event. One can imagine his fear when he heard from the wise men that the sign had come.

To protect himself, Herod ordered that all the children of Bethlehem and the surrounding area who were under two years old should be killed by his soldiers. It was once thought that hundreds, even thousands, of children had been slaughtered in the massacre. But recent research has greatly reduced this number. In fact, some experts think that fewer than twenty children in that age group would have been living in Bethlehem and its neighbourhood at the time.

The Flight to Egypt

We are told in Matthew's Gospel that the Holy Family had fled to Egypt because they had been warned of

The shepherd was an important figure in biblical times. Jesus, seen here, was often described as the Good Shepherd.

Herod's intention to harm the baby Jesus. While they were in Egypt Herod died, but Mary and Joseph were too frightened to return to their homeland because they knew that Herod's son, Archelaus, was now King of Judaea. They had good reason to be fearful. Archelaus was immediately faced with a Jewish revolt. With the same ruthlessness as his father, he sent his troops into Jerusalem and in a single day slaughtered 3000 Jews.

Jewish celebrations

There were many chances for celebration in Palestine at the time of Jesus. In addition to Jewish religious festivals such as Passover, Rosh Hashanah and Hanukkah, there would have been weddings, harvests, sheep-shearings, even funerals, where some kind of feast was provided. And, of course, there were birthdays. Many are recorded in the Old Testament, but only one in the New Testament. Unfortunately it ended with the beheading of John the Baptist.

Religious laws forbid the Jews to eat certain kinds of food. Foods that can be eaten are said to be *kosher* which is a Hebrew word meaning 'correct or proper'. Prohibited foods are *treyfar*, which is Hebrew for 'unfit', and they include pork products and shellfish such as shrimp and lobster. Animals whose meat may be eaten must be killed in a special way and according to strict religious rules. Meat and dairy products cannot be eaten together for, as the Old Testament says, 'Seethe not the kid in its mother's milk'.

A modern folk artist's painting of Passover, one of the most important of Jewish religious festivals.

Food and drink

If we look at the food served today in such countries as Morocco, Algeria, and Tunisia, we get a good idea of what people at the time of Jesus might have eaten.

There was plenty of fruit such as figs, dates, grapes, pomegranates, and melons, but none of the oranges, lemons, and grapefruit for which the lands bordering the Mediterranean are nowadays famous. These citrus fruits were not introduced into the Holy Land until many centuries after Christ.

Nuts included pistachios and almonds, and among a wide range of vegetables were onions, garlic, lentils, beans, cucumbers, and leeks. Dishes were often flavoured with herbs such as mint, dill, cumin, and mustard. Honey was used a great deal in cooking because there was no sugar in this part of the world until it was introduced into the Middle East in the fourteenth and fifteenth centuries.

Bread-making was always the responsibility of women. In this Victorian illustration the dough is being kneaded by the mother while her daughter carries a loaf to the oven.

In most ordinary families such as the one in which Jesus lived, meat, generally in the form of lamb or goat, would have been served only on special occasions, for none but the wealthy could afford it regularly. Fish, chicken and eggs were eaten instead. Locusts and grasshoppers, which are plentiful in the Holy Land and full of nutritious protein, were a special treat, especially grilled over charcoal, which made them deliciously crunchy.

To accompany a meal, wine was preferred to water, if only because it was safer to drink. Pure water was not easy to come by since the main sources, rivers and streams, were shared with animals and used both for washing and sewage. Sometimes, on particularly festive occasions, a very strong drink, made from corn, honey, and dates, was served.

Cooking

Most homes had an oven in an open yard near the house. The oven was a clay dome about 3 feet (1 metre) high with an air-hole in the side to help the fire burn and an opening at the front for the fuel, usually wood, thorn branches and dried animal droppings. It was rather like the *tandoor* oven used today in many parts of India.

A flat, unleavened kind of bread, very much like modern pita bread, was the essential part of every meal. The baking of bread was a daily ritual of the greatest importance. It was the responsibility of the women of the family who heated the oven, stuck the dough to the inside of the oven wall and left it until it browned. Once baked, the bread was plucked off the wall with a stick.

Stews were very popular. They were made by mixing meat with fruit and cooking everything slowly in a large clay pot—a cooking recipe that was later brought back to Europe by knights returning from the Crusades in the Holy Land and one that is still very popular today in the Middle East.

One dish, many hands

It was the custom at the time of Jesus, as it still is among many families in the Middle East, for everyone to eat from one shared dish. In those days only men sat down to the meal, squatting on the floor around a great bowl heaped with food. Women were there to serve and they were expected to keep in the background and only allowed to eat their food away from the main eating area after the men had finished.

After first washing their hands, each person would tear off a large piece of flat bread for scooping up the food. It was important to use only the right hand as the left was considered unclean. There were no knives or forks or individual plates.

When the feast was over, the older men would tell the legends and myths of their people. Familiar songs would be sung. For the young boys present, this was a chance to hear about the customs and traditions of their tribes and societies. In this way, the history of the people was passed from generation to generation.

The first Christmases

Although the early Christians had decided to use the same time of year as their pagan rivals to celebrate the birth of their Saviour, they were careful not to borrow too many pagan habits. 'We hold this day holy,' said one Christian, 'not like the pagans because of the birth of the sun, but because of Him who made it.'

Their celebration, therefore, was to be quite solemn, a feast or 'mass' in honour of Christ's birthday. As we have seen, 'Christmas' is 'Cristes maesse'. And the Latin *missa* means to send away, as on a mission. Those leaving the mass were thought to be on God's mission.

Missa also means bread, which represents the body of Christ and was offered as such by Jesus to his disciples at the Last Supper.

We still use the old word 'maesse' or 'mess' in the sense of a meal when we refer to the room where soldiers, sailors, and air force personnel eat. So when we sit down to our Christmas meal, there is an echo of the early Christian mass: the celebration feast.

Celebrating mass

Because early Christmases were celebrations of mass, they would hardly have been noisy parties, nor would they have been centred on a big feast. About 100 years after Christ, the mass had stopped being an actual meal and had simply become a symbol of a

The mass is a symbolic meal where worshippers come together to celebrate their faith. The word 'Christmas' means coming together to celebrate the birth of Christ.

meal. The bread and wine stood for all the other foods and drink. The mass of the early Christians probably took place in homes and simple chapels rather than in churches as we know them. In fact, three masses were, and still are, held: the first at midnight on Christmas Eve, the second at dawn on Christmas Day, and the third a few hours later, at midday. The most popular was the midnight mass, probably begun in the reign of Pope Sixtus III about 430 years after Christ. The Pope converted a pagan temple into the church of Santa Maria Maggiore in Rome and held midnight mass over the crypt.

3

CHRISTMAS LONG AGO

Medieval celebrations

Most historians agree that the medieval period, often called the Middle Ages, lasted roughly a thousand years, from about the late fifth century to the fifteenth century. Strictly speaking, it was not a distinct period with a beginning and an end, but the terms are used broadly to describe the time in European history that followed the collapse of the Roman Empire and preceded the exciting new achievements in art, literature, science, and discovery that became known as the Renaissance.

A time to rest and be merry

If Easter was the most solemn of the medieval holidays, Christmas was the happiest and longest, lasting from Christmas Eve until the Feast of Epiphany on 6 January.

The long Christmas holiday was enjoyed by rich and poor alike, with as much food and drink as each could afford. During the two weeks of Christmas farm workers, as well as their animals, were given a holiday. Naturally, it was in the royal, noble and wealthy households that Christmas was celebrated in fullest splendour.

◄ A French illustration of the fifteenth century shows the sort of feast a wealthy family might have enjoyed at Christmas.

Λ The traditional Christmas boar's head is carried into the Great Hall, announced by trumpeters and singers.

V The wassail bowls are being filled and shared; the Christmas pie waits to be opened, and even the dog enjoys its Christmas treat.

Preparing the Christmas feast

Because Christmas was the biggest feast of the year, preparations had to be made as early as November. First, pigs and cattle had to be killed. It was necessary to do this in any case because there was usually not enough animal feed to keep them through the winter. Every part of the animal was used and nothing was wasted.

Meat was prevented from going bad in a number of ways. Sometimes it was rubbed with a blend of salt and spices, sometimes it was pickled in a mixture of vinegar and spices, or it might just be left hanging in the smoky fireplace until it was preserved or 'cured'.

Even for poorer families, Christmas was a time of activity in the kitchen. If you were lucky, as here, your lord might bring you Christmas gifts.

The Great Pie of Sir Henry Grey

The list of ingredients that went into a pie made for Sir Henry Grey in 1430 gives some idea as to why it was called 'great'. The pie was 9 feet (3 metres) in circumference and weighed 165 pounds (73 kilograms). It contained:

20 lbs (9 kg) of butter	6 snipe
4 geese	4 partridges
2 rabbits	2 ox tongues
4 ducks	2 curlews
2 woodcock	6 pigeons
	7 blackbirds

Fruit was extremely popular and used in many dishes. So, following the autumn harvest, apples, pears, plums, quinces, and other fruits were dried in order to be stored throughout the winter.

'A Great Pye'

The few days before Christmas saw tremendous activity in the kitchen. One of the first tasks was to make a huge pastry case for a pie. Great quantities of beef and lamb were then ground up together and salt and pepper added. This mixture was called 'forcemeat', a word that comes from the French word *farci*, meaning 'stuffed' or 'filled'.

The forcemeat was placed in the bottom of the pie. Next came boiled hens, rabbits, ducks and any game birds that were available, such as partridges or woodcock. They were first boned and then laid on top of the forcemeat. After these came another layer of

32

forcemeat, and above that chopped marrow, the yolks of hard-boiled eggs, currants, prunes, and dates. Now was the time to add some favourite spices such as mace, cloves, cinnamon, and saffron. Finally, a pastry lid was put on the pie and the whole thing baked. Sometimes the finished product was so big that the pastry case had to be held together by iron bands!

The 'umble' pie

In an age when hunting deer was the favourite sport of the nobleman, the 'umble' pie was a popular dish. It was made from the 'umbles' of the deer, that is the heart, liver, tongue, feet, brains, and ears. The umbles were mixed with stewing beef, bacon, oysters, and rabbit or hare. On top of all these meats was a layer

Venison, the meat of the deer, was highly prized in the Middle Ages. Even the deer's innards or 'umbles' went into the famous 'umble pie'.

King Henry III of England, seen here, sometimes threw lavish Christmas feasts but expected others to pay for them.

of dried fruit. The whole rich mixture was then put in a pastry case and baked.

This tasty dish, however, was not destined to end up in front of the lords, ladies, and their guests. They ate the best part of the deer, the flesh. The left-overs that went to make up the 'umble' pie were only considered suitable for the huntsmen and the servants. This is why the phrase 'to eat humble pie' means that someone who has come down in life is forced to give way to those in higher positions and be made humble, or humiliated.

Royal entertainment

Kings and nobles in the Middle Ages were expected to provide lavish Christmas entertainment. By doing so they showed their power and wealth, and it gave them the chance to reward the people who supported them. They would give expensive presents, too, to their knights and household staff—fine clothes, per-

The pre-Christmas boar hunt provided the nobles with grand Christmas dishes such as boar's head.

derstanding it. At that moment a great wild boar sprang out of the undergrowth and charged. As cool as a cucumber, the quick-thinking scholar took his book, and rammed it down the boar's throat, saying, 'Swallow that if you can!' The boar choked on the book and died.

The Queen's College feast starts with the cooked boar's head, decorated with rosemary, bay, and holly, being carried by four men into the great hall. A fifth man, who heads the procession, sings the traditional 'Boar's Head Carol' dating from the fourteenth century, the first verse of which goes:

> The boar's head in hand bear I
> Bedecked with bays and rosemary
> And I pray you, my masters, be merry
> *Quot est is in convivio**

*As many as are at the feast

Frumenty: the original Christmas pudding?

Our Christmas pudding has its origins in a dish enjoyed in the Middle Ages by both rich and poor: the spicy porridge called frumenty.

The first stage in making frumenty was to boil wheat in water until it turned into a soft porridge or gruel. To this was added milk, currants and other dried fruit. Then the yolks of eggs were mixed in, together with spices such as nutmeg and cinnamon. Finally, the frumenty mixture was cooked into a kind of stiff pudding.

In some Scandinavian countries such as Sweden and Norway, porridge is still part of a traditional Christmas meal.

Wassail: the Christmas punch

Another important element of the Christmas feast was a strong drink consisting of ale, nutmeg, honey, and ginger known as wassail. The host would pick up the wassail bowl and greet his companions with 'waes hael', the Old English words for 'be well'. The guests would reply 'drinc hael', meaning 'drink and be well'. Then the bowl would be passed around the table.

On top of the punch, pieces of toasted bread were floated. The first person to be offered the wassail bowl would take out the first piece of toast and wish the company good health. And it is from this tradi-

'Tis well to be merry - 'tis well to be gay - May you be both Dear, this bright Christmas Day.

MERRY CHRISTMAS GREETINGS.

The Christmas pudding evolved from the medieval spicy porridge called 'frumenty'.

A steaming wassail bowl complete with bobbing apples about to burst open and spread their 'lamb's wool' across the surface of the hot punch.

tion that we get our expression, 'to raise or make a toast'.

Sometimes baked apples were dropped into the bowl of punch. As they burst in the hot liquid they would spread apple pulp over the surface of the drink, and this was known as 'lamb's wool'.

Christmas in the medieval village

Ordinary villagers in the Middle Ages welcomed the two weeks of Christmas as the highlight of the year. It was a time to celebrate the birth of Christ and to look forward to the coming of spring. The villagers

Villagers (here seen at work in a fifteenth-century illustration) could look forward
to a time of rest at Christmas.

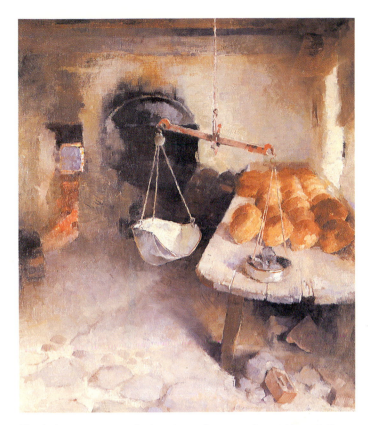

The bakery was not only the place where you bought bread. For a few pennies the baker would also cook your meat and pies.

were given time off by their lord from working on his lands, and in any event, frost, snow and heavy winter rains often made it difficult for them to work out in the fields. Christmas was one of those rare occasions when the villagers had time to enjoy themselves. If they were fortunate, they received annual gifts such as ale, food, firewood, or clothing.

Most of the poorer farm-workers lived on what they could get from the land and hedgerows. There were eggs, oats for making porridge, cheese perhaps, and maybe rabbits and pigeons. If a pig had been killed in the autumn, there might be smoked ham at Christmas and plenty of ale or cider to drink.

Sometimes the more important farmers who rented land were invited to the great hall for a Christmas treat. According to one account, this is what they might have been given:

'... two white loaves, as much beer as they will drink in a day, a mess [dish] of beef and bacon with mustard, one brewis [stew] of hen, and a cheese, fuel to cook their food, and two candles to burn from dinnertime until even afterwards.'

If you were lower down the social scale, you might still get an invitation, but you would be expected to bring your own cup and trencher, candles, and cooking fuel. You were allowed, however, to take away any food you could not eat—a sort of medieval doggy-bag.

Christmas in town

'Every man's house, as also their parish churches, was decked with holly, ivy, bay, and whatsoever of the season of the year afforded to be green.'

William Fitzstephen, writing in the twelfth century about London at Christmas.

If you lived in a medieval town you probably would not own proper cooking equipment. Homes were often cramped and most people took their meat and pies to the baker. For a small charge, the baker put your dish in his oven and cooked it. This system was common among many poorer people until the end of the nineteenth century. And in some country districts of Italy, Greece, and Spain, for example, it is still used.

Other items of the Christmas dinner could be bought locally. There were many shops selling ready-to-eat food, and prices were controlled by the Church. For example, in the fourteenth century you could have bought your Christmas goose already cooked for sevenpence. If you bought it raw, it cost sixpence.

Entertainments

After the feasting everyone joined in the games. One was called 'hot cockles'. A person was blindfolded and knelt down. The others then hit the blindfolded player, who had to guess their names in turn. 'Hot cockles' remained popular up to the Victorian age. Here is how one player in the eighteenth century described it in a letter to a newspaper:

'I am a footman in a great family and am in love with the housemaid. We were at hot cockles last night in the hall these Christmas holidays. When I lay down and was blindfolded she pulled off her shoe and hit me with the heel such a rap as almost broke my head to pieces. Pray, Sir, was this love or spite?'

39

Blind Man's Buff was a favourite Christmas game
from the Middle Ages until the Age of TV.

Another game played in the Middle Ages was 'hoodman blind', which we now know as 'blind man's buff'. In those days men wore hoods as part of their clothing. The hood was turned around to cover the eyes so that the wearer could not see. He then had to try to catch one of the other players.

Morris dancers

Morris dancing was very popular at Christmas, especially in England. This type of dance was thought to have started in Spain when it was ruled by the Arabs or Moors: and from 'Moors' came 'Morris'.

The dancers wore colourful costumes covered in ribbons and little bells. Morris dancing had almost died out by the early part of the present century but now many groups have revived this ancient custom.

Mummers

Mumming plays were greatly enjoyed in the Middle Ages but they probably go back to the days of the Saturnalia festivities of ancient Rome, which would have reached Britain when the country was occupied by the Romans.

Mummers' plays could be seen all over Europe, although each country would have slightly different characters. The words were passed down from generation to generation, and over the centuries they became a bit jumbled. For example, this peculiar little verse in the Marshfield mummers' play in England has nothing whatsoever to do with the plot.

'There is a house on yonder hill,
So high I do declare,
'Twas on a cold and winter's night,
My grandmother left me there.'

Mummers were a traditional part of Christmas entertainment from the Middle Ages until the beginning of this century.

In England, the plot usually concerned the central character of St George, who, as the nation's patron saint, stood for Christianity. He would have a fight with a Turk, the traditional enemy of Christians. When St George was killed, the audience would boo, whistle and hiss at the Turk, just as we greet the villain at the pantomime. Along would come the Good Doctor and bring St George back to life. The audience now had a chance to cheer and shout. And there were other characters intended to make them laugh, as, for instance, a man dressed up in women's clothes and a fool with his cap and bells.

Mumming today

The old mumming plays almost died out in England with the First World War. With so many young men killed in France, there were too few left to learn and continue the old traditions.

Today, however, some of the old mumming plays have been revived. For example, at Gloucester on Boxing Day you can see two plays: the 'Gloucester Play', which takes place in the grounds of the cathedral, and the 'Bisley Play', held at the New Inn Courtyard. There are also Christmas mumming plays performed at Moulton in Northamptonshire, at Marshfield near Bristol, at Crookham in Hampshire, and at Greatham in Cleveland.

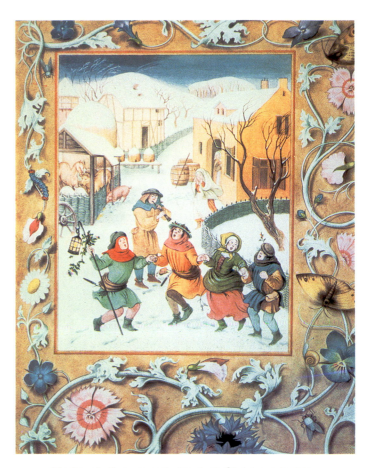

Medieval villagers enjoying their Christmas holiday.

Mummers: medieval Christmas clowns

The word 'mummer' comes from an Old French word, *momer*, meaning 'to go masked'. The costumes worn by mummers in the Middle Ages were very odd indeed. For example, some of the mummers who entertained King Edward III of England in 1347 dressed as rabbits, while one was got up as a bunch of legs waving in the air!

The modern clown owes a great deal to the comic mummers of the Middle Ages.

In America, one of the great Christmas traditions is the Philadelphia Mummers' Parade which takes place on New Year's Day. The parade, started just over 100 years ago, has now grown into an enormous procession of floats, mumming groups, marching bands, and other forms of entertainment.

Mystery plays

The medieval 'Mystery' play was not a crime story, as we would understand it today. It was a street performance that set out to describe the meaning of the Bible stories. The most popular of these plays were those about the Christmas story.

Mysteries began as religious processions or pageants. In those days, groups of merchants or craftsmen banded together to form associations known as guilds—from the word 'gild', meaning 'payment' or 'offering'.

Each of a town's merchant guilds paid for a beautifully decorated cart or float. For example, the goldsmiths' guild paid for the float that showed the arrival of the Magi at the stable of the inn in Bethlehem. The thatchers (the craftsmen who put thatch or reeds on roofs) were responsible for the float that showed the infant Jesus inside the stable, which was, of course, suitably thatched.

Each float was manned, not by professional actors, but by guild members who posed as the characters of the Nativity. Gradually words were added and little plays were performed. The wagons or floats often had impressive stage effects such as flying angels, fire-breathing monsters, and trapdoors.

The Mystery Cycles

The Mystery plays were performed in groups of plays called 'cycles'. The most famous ones in England were the Chester, Coventry, York, and Wakefield Cycles. Each cycle could last a very long time, and as people poured in from the countryside to see the plays, the town hummed with the bustle, activity, and excitement of the marketplace, much to the delight and profit of the merchants who paid for the performances.

The York Cycle, for example, was made up of forty-eight plays which started at 4.30 in the morning and lasted all day. The Chester Cycle had twenty-five plays and lasted three days. And in France there were Mystery cycles that had 500 speaking parts, 60,000 lines and took forty days to complete!

Clowns and villains

The crowds who watched the medieval Mystery plays enjoyed good slapstick comedy. Their particular favourites were the three shepherds of the Nativity story—Hanken, Harvey, and Tudde. These clownish characters were not too bright and spent their time arguing about what exactly the angel of the Lord had said to them. They would tease one another, wrestle, and generally play the fool. These dim-witted shepherds, nevertheless, were kind-hearted folk and they gave their own humble gifts to the infant Jesus: a bottle without a stopper, a cup, a pair of gloves, a ball, and an old spoon.

In contrast, Herod was the character in the Mystery play whom everyone loved to hate. He would growl, snort, scream, and run around the audience. Children were terrified, especially when they saw the Massacre of the Innocents. Realistic-looking dummies were

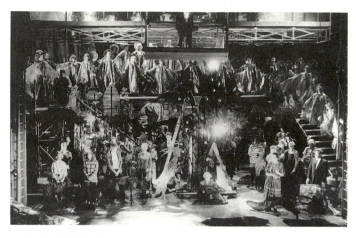

In the Middle Ages Mystery Plays could last for three days.

used, with lots of pretend blood. Everyone cheered when old Herod was dragged down to Hell through a trapdoor out of which billowed real smoke. Justice had been done and the audience could go home with the satisfying memory of Herod's agonizing screams echoing from under the floorboards of the stage.

A supernatural Christmas

The adventure story of Sir Gawain and the Green Knight was written over 600 years ago and is one of

King Arthur's Round Table: the setting for the opening of 'Sir Gawain and the Green Knight', a medieval supernatural Christmas story.

the oldest and most mysterious Christmas tales in the English language.

It is Christmas time at Camelot. King Arthur and his queen, Guinevere, together with the knights of the Round Table and their ladies, are enjoying their feast: 'A noble din by day, dancing at night.'

Just before the meal, King Arthur announces that he will not eat until he has heard a 'marvel', which in those days meant a story of amazing acts of bravery and daring, or weird and wonderful happenings. No sooner has the king spoken than a giant enters the hall. His skin, his long hair and his bushy beard are a ghostly green colour. Clad in a great fur-lined coat, in one hand he carries a bunch of holly, in the other an enormous axe. The assembled guests are speechless with amazement and fear.

The Green Knight challenges the king and his knights to a terrifying 'Christmas game'. He will allow any knight to strike him once with his huge axe: but on one condition. 'If I survive your blow,' he declares, 'I must be allowed to return the blow one year from this day at a place of my choosing—the Green Chapel.'

The brave young Sir Gawain accepts the challenge, swings the mighty axe and cuts off the giant's head. But to everyone's horror, the Green Knight, instead of falling down dead, coolly picks up his head and remounts his horse. Head in hand, he reminds Sir Gawain that at Christmas in one year's time he must come to the Green Chapel to receive a blow from the giant's axe.

Sir Gawain and Sir Bertilak

Bound by the strict rules of knightly chivalry, Sir Gawain sets out next Christmas for the Green Chapel. On the way he is given shelter in a castle by its lord, Sir Bertilak, and his beautiful wife.

Sir Bertilak proposes his own Christmas game. He offers to give everything he kills during three days' hunting to Sir Gawain, if, in return, the young knight hands over to his host everything he is given while staying at the castle. Gawain agrees.

On the first two days of the hunt, Bertilak's wife, a little friendlier than a good wife should be, kisses Gawain, who duly returns the kisses to her husband. On the third day she gives him a green belt and makes him promise not to tell anyone of her gift. What is Gawain to do? As an honourable knight he cannot

betray a lady. But what of his agreement with Bertilak? He chooses to say nothing and leaves for the Green Chapel.

The time for reckoning

At the chapel, where he meets the Green Knight, everything is dark, cold, and gloomy. Gawain is sure he is about to be killed. The giant raises his axe but, astonishingly, only pretends to strike Gawain. He raises the axe again and the blade whistles past Gawain's head. The third blow of the huge weapon merely nicks Gawain's neck, just enough to make him bleed slightly.

Gawain is amazed, wondering why he has been spared. All is soon revealed. The Green Knight is Sir Bertilak in another form. He has known all along that Sir Gawain has broken his word by not giving up the green belt, but judging it to be only a small fault, has decided that a slight wound is the rightful punishment. Gawain is ashamed, but returns to Camelot to be greeted as a hero.

The meaning of the poem

In the fourteenth century, when this great poem was written, a battle of ideas was still being fought between the old Norse pagan myths and the newer Christian teaching. Some people believe that the Green Knight stands for pagan magic. He is described as having a great beard, wearing a fur-lined coat and riding a horse. This was just how Odin, the Norse god, was often depicted. Sir Gawain, on the other hand, represents Christianity. He cannot be killed by the Green Knight because he is protected by his faith.

On another level, the poem is about the struggle between the seasons. The Green Knight stands for the forces of winter. He carries holly, a winter plant, and he lives in the cold, dark north. Sir Gawain, however, comes from the sunny, warm south, and at one point is described as 'looking like spring'. Christmas is the time when spring is about to defeat winter.

Twelfth Night

Epiphany or Twelfth Night, 6 January, is the traditional end of the Christmas holiday, the date on which we take down the tree and the decorations. To do so earlier is thought to bring bad luck for the rest

Twelfth Night or Epiphany, celebrated on 6 January, marks the day Jesus was shown to the outside world.
The word 'Epiphany' is from the Greek 'to show'.

of the year. From the Middle Ages until the mid-nineteenth century, Twelfth Night was almost more popular than Christmas Day, and even today Eastern Orthodox churches celebrate Epiphany as the most important day of the Christmas season.

During the Middle Ages, on Twelfth Night, kings would take part in a special ceremony, dressed in their finest robes. In 1330 King Edward I of England made offerings of frankincense, gold, and myrrh in his royal chapel. Until the reign of George III in the eighteenth century, the monarch always attended this ceremony. The service is still held at the Chapel Royal of St James's Palace in London, but now the monarch is not present in person, and the old gifts of spices have been replaced by special coins.

The meaning of Epiphany

'Epiphany' comes from a Greek word which means 'to show'. For Christians, it marked the 'showing' of Jesus to the outside world when he was visited by the Magi. Like many Christian celebrations, it has its roots in the ancient world. In the Egypt of the Pharaohs, 6 January was a sacred day to mark the overflowing of the River Nile which flooded its banks about this time each year and made the land fertile again.

The Twelfth Night party was traditionally the most boisterous of the year.

A fourteenth-century painting showing St Nicholas of Myra (the original Santa Claus) giving a dowry to the daughters of a poor man.

Cakes and ale

Twelfth Night was the occasion for the best party of the year, when everyone went slightly crazy. And one person was chosen to lead the craziness. On the day beforehand a special cake was prepared. A dried bean was put in the dough and the cake was baked. If you found the bean in your piece of cake you were declared 'King of the Bean' and put in charge of the whole party.

Nothing went down better at the Twelfth Night party than a good joke. One of the favourites was a surprise pie. First, a very large amount of pastry was prepared and baked as an empty pie case. Holes were cut in the bottom and live birds and frogs were put inside the pie. Then, as the old nursery rhyme says, 'When the pie was opened, the birds began to sing.'

It was a tradition on Twelfth Night, too, for farmers to 'wassail' their orchards, carrying a bowl of punch or cider to the apple trees and pouring a little of the drink on the trees' roots. This, it was hoped, would bring a good harvest in the coming year.

Christmas saints

Of all the saints associated with Christmas, perhaps the best loved is St Nicholas. He is particularly popular in Russia, France, Germany, Luxembourg, Switzerland, Belgium and Holland, and there are probably more churches named after him in Europe than any other saint.

St Nicholas' Day is celebrated on 6 December and marks the day of his death about the year 343. Nicholas was born into a wealthy family in the province

St Nicholas was the patron saint of sailors, as well as of children and pawnbrokers.

of Lycia, and eventually became bishop of the town of Myra. Both of these places are in what is now Turkey.

The legend of St Nicholas: chimneys and stockings

The young Nicholas once met a very poor man who was in despair because he did not have enough money to give his three daughters a marriage dowry. A dowry is a payment that the family of a daughter was expected to make to the family of the husband-to-be, and without it she could not be married. As there was no money to feed and clothe the girls, the terrible prospect loomed of their being sold into slavery.

Nicholas had just inherited his parents' fortune. He wanted to help the unfortunate father but, being a modest man, he did not wish to draw attention to himself. So, on three successive nights, Nicholas climbed on to the poor man's roof and dropped a bag of gold down the chimney. The girls had hung their freshly washed stockings in the fireplace to dry, and into each stocking plopped a fat bag of gold—enough for a dowry and the prospect of marriage. Ever afterwards, chimneys and stockings were to find a special place in the Christmas tradition.

Patron saint of children, sailors— and pawnbrokers

Known for his generosity and particular concern for the young, St Nicholas became the patron saint of children. Moreover, because of a series of miracles he had performed while on board a merchant ship taking him on a pilgrimage to the Holy Land, he was also the patron saint of seafarers. In later centuries, the owners of these ships would paint three bags of gold on the sides of their vessels. The sign was meant to represent the three gifts Nicholas had given to the daughters of the poor man of Patras, and the merchants hoped, therefore, that his spirit would protect their ships.

In the Middle Ages people would often borrow money from merchants. Over the years, the sign of the three bags became simpler and eventually turned into three balls—the emblem of the pawnbroker or moneylender. And so St Nicholas also came to be venerated as the patron saint of pawnbrokers.

Later still, as we shall see, St Nicholas turned into Santa Claus.

St Stephen: the first Christian martyr

Stephen, like Jesus, was Jewish. Little is known of his early life, but he spoke Greek and was probably born and raised in the great city of Alexandria, in Egypt. Stephen was chosen by the twelve disciples of Jesus to help spread the good news of Christianity.

In Jerusalem, while he was arguing the Christian faith, Stephen was reported to the Sanhedrin, the highest court of the Jewish people. He was accused of speaking against Moses and God. Stephen attacked the members of the court in strong terms, calling them 'stiffnecked' for resisting the Holy Ghost. Furious with anger at Stephen's accusations, the court immediately ordered him to be taken outside and stoned to death. As he lay dying, Stephen

A sixteenth-century painting of the first Christian martyr, St Stephen, who is celebrated in the West on 26 December, in the East on 27 December.

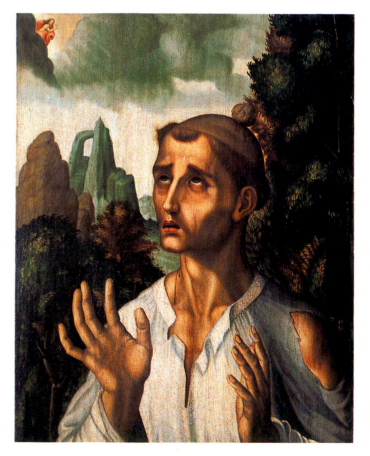

The legend of the wrens

An old Irish legend says that Stephen was first put in prison by the Sanhedrin. He would have escaped but his guards were woken by the chirping of wrens. Thereafter, on 26 December, wrens were stoned to death in Ireland and other parts of Britain in a ceremony called 'The Wren Massacre'. The wrens' bodies were tied to poles and paraded around the houses by groups of young boys who would knock on doors and ask for money. In exchange, the boys would hand over a wren feather, which was considered a lucky charm. Thankfully, this cruel Christmas custom died out during the 1920s.

St John: son of thunder

John and his brother James were fishermen, and it was while they were mending their fishing nets on the Sea of Galilee that Jesus called them to join him and become his disciples. John and James were not educated men and both of them were rough and tough. Once, for example, when a town refused to let Jesus enter, the brothers offered to burn it down. Jesus called the pair of them the 'sons of thunder'.

John took special care of the Virgin Mary after Jesus' crucifixion, and later he travelled widely. John ended his life at Ephesus, in what is now Turkey, at a very old age. He was the only one of the disciples not to die violently.

The feast day of St John is celebrated by the Roman Catholic Church on 27 December and by the Eastern Orthodox Church on 8 May.

Good King Wenceslas

Wenceslas was one of the first Christian kings of Bohemia, now a part of modern Czechoslovakia. During a time of great unrest in his country, Wenceslas tried to govern according to Christian teaching. However, he could not prevent the invasion of Bohemia by German tribes and he was killed by Bohemians who thought he was too weak. Those who plotted against him included his own mother, Drahomir, and his brother, Boleslas.

We tend to associate Wenceslas with 26 December because, the carol tells us, it was 'on the feast of Stephen' that the good king went gathering fuel for his poor subjects. In fact, St Wenceslas' Day is 28 September, for that was the day in 949 that he was

Although King Wenceslas is usually shown as an older man, he was only twenty-two years old when he was murdered.

prayed for his murderers. One man in the crowd of onlookers was Saul of Tarsus, who had held the coats of the stone-throwers. The sight of the murder moved him so deeply that it helped convert him to Christianity. Saul eventually became the great apostle St Paul.

We do not know the exact date on which Stephen was put to death, but it was probably around the year 35. The Church decided to make 26 December Stephen's day as a special honour to the first follower of Jesus to die for his beliefs. The Eastern Orthodox Church celebrates St Stephen's Day on 27 December.

St Thomas à Becket was killed by knights of King Henry II on 29 December 1170.

murdered. And although the saint is often depicted as an older man with grey hair, Wenceslas, in fact, was only twenty-two when he died.

St Thomas à Becket

Thomas à Becket was born in London in 1118. As a young man he entered the Church and quickly progressed. King Henry II recognized his talent, and by the age of thirty-six, Becket had become Chancellor of England.

In 1162 Becket was made Archbishop of Canterbury. Then his relations with the king turned sour. Henry demanded that the Church give up certain traditional rights and Thomas, as head of the Church, refused. Former friendship changed to bitter rivalry.

One day, in a fit of rage, King Henry ranted, 'Who will rid me of this turbulent priest?' Four of his knights took the king at his word and set off for Canterbury.

In the late afternoon of 29 December 1170, the knights arrived at the cathedral and demanded that Becket give in to the royal demands. When the archbishop refused, the knights started to break down the cathedral doors. Becket told his frightened priests

that 'a cathedral is not a castle', and himself opened the doors. The knights rushed in, shouting, 'Where is Thomas the traitor? Where is the archbishop?' Becket replied, 'Here I am, no traitor, but archbishop and priest of God.'

One of the knights grabbed Thomas and tried to drag him out of the cathedral, because to harm someone in a sacred place was a terrible sin, but Thomas threw him to the ground. Two of the others then struck and wounded Becket with their swords. While the archbishop lay bleeding, the fourth knight delivered an enormous blow which split his skull. The knights then ran from the scene of their crime.

When the news reached the king, he is said to have shut himself up and fasted for forty days. Later, he did public penance for his part in Becket's murder.

Feast of the Holy Innocents

In medieval times the name given to the day of the Holy Innocents, 28 December, was 'Childermass', to commemorate the massacre of the children by Herod in Bethlehem. In some European countries it was considered a very unlucky day, when no marriages were held, no legal contracts were made, and no new building was started. King Edward IV of England, for example, even put off his coronation because it fell on Childermass day.

According to an old English custom, all children had to be beaten on Holy Innocents' Day to remind them of Herod's terrible deed. Luckily this painful Christmas whacking died out about 250 years ago!

Throughout Europe there was a tradition of beating children on Holy Innocents' Day (28 December). It was meant to remind them of Herod's Massacre of the Innocents.

The Boy Bishop

Children had a happier time in those parts of Europe where Holy Innocents' Day was celebrated as the climax of the Christmas season. On 6 December, St Nicholas' Day, a boy was chosen to be the 'Boy Bishop'. His big moment came on Holy Innocents' Day when he was dressed in the gorgeous ceremonial robes of the bishop and seated on the bishop's throne. For the whole day he and his friends were in full charge. He had to give a sermon and bless the people. At the end of the day he and his companions were given a feast and showered with gifts and money. This custom lasted until the seventeenth century.

Christmas plants

When we decorate our homes with holly and ivy and other plants, we are observing a tradition that goes back to ancient times.

The plants most commonly used in early Christmas festivities were evergreens, the leaves of which stay green all year round. Some, like holly and mistletoe, not only have green leaves throughout the winter but also bear fruit in the form of berries. When Nature seemed to be dead, these plants were very much alive. So, for our ancestors, evergreen plants represented the promise of spring and renewed life. We have already seen the important part mistletoe played in the lives and religious rituals of the Druids.

Holly

Although the word 'holly' seems remarkably close to the word 'holy', it simply comes from an Old English word, *holen*. Holly has been a favourite winter plant for thousands of years. The ancient Romans gave sprigs of holly as gifts. The Druids, too, believed that good spirits lived in its branches and would take sprigs into their homes for luck and prosperity. Holly was also said to keep evil spirits away. In Scandinavia, especially, it was traditional for unmarried

Decorating a house with holly, ivy, fir, and other greenery goes back to the ancient Greeks and Romans.

The ancient Romans and Druids used holly in their winter solstice celebrations.

The god Bacchus wearing ivy. Bacchus was the ancient Roman god of feasting and drinking, and because of these pagan associations ivy was not used by the early Christian Church.

Ivy, laurel, and rosemary

In ancient Rome ivy was the badge of Bacchus, the god of feasting and drinking. Because of this pagan association, the early Christian Church would not allow ivy to be used for decoration. In the Middle Ages people thought it helped them to recognize witches, and it was also said to be a protection against the deadly plague.

The laurel tree is also known as bay. The ancient Greeks and Romans used its leaves as a crown of victory. Laurel was also probably the first plant to be used by early Christians to decorate their churches.

Rosemary is an evergreen herb often used in cooking, but it also has a special meaning at Christmas. Legend says that when Mary, Joseph, and the baby Jesus fled into Egypt, Mary washed the baby's clothes and spread them out to dry over a rosemary bush, so that they became beautifully scented.

In the Middle Ages rosemary was thought to be a good protection against evil spirits.

The Glastonbury thorn

The old abbey at Glastonbury in Somerset is now only a ruin, but for many hundreds of years it has been a holy place. The site of King Arthur's Camelot is said to be near by and some say that Arthur and his queen,

women to tie sprigs to their beds to avoid being turned into witches.

Some early Christians thought holly stood for Moses' Burning Bush, with the berries representing flames. Holly was also connected with the Crown of Thorns Christ was made to wear at his crucifixion. Legend says that the berries were originally white but were turned red by Christ's blood. In pagan times holly was believed to be male, but in Christianity it was associated with the Virgin Mary.

Poinsettia: a favourite Christmas plant

The brilliant red poinsettia is named after Joel Roberts Poinsett, who was sent as American ambassador to Mexico in 1825. He saw the flower being used there as a Christmas decoration, where it was known as 'the flower of the Holy Night'. Mr Poinsett brought some plants back to the United States. A century or so later, professional growers in California began to sell the plant at Christmas and it quickly became popular. Today the industry that grows poinsettias for the Christmas market is enormous and has spread to many countries of the world.

Glastonbury Abbey in Somerset, England, is the home of the legendary Glastonbury thorn.

Joseph of Arimathea allowed his family tomb to be used for Christ's burial. Here he looks on as the door of the tomb is sealed. Joseph was sent to Britain in AD 63 and was said to have founded the first Christian settlement at Glastonbury Abbey.

Guinevere, are buried in the abbey grounds. Even today the ruins have a magical atmosphere.

An old legend tells of the time when Glastonbury was visited by Joseph of Arimathea. Joseph had been close to Jesus, and it was in Joseph's family tomb that the body of Christ was laid after the crucifixion. The legend relates how the apostle Philip sent Joseph to England in AD 63 to found the first Christian settlement, at Glastonbury. Joseph was supposed to have brought with him the Holy Grail, the cup from which Jesus had drunk at the Last Supper with his disciples. When Joseph arrived at Glastonbury, he is said to have plunged his walking staff, made from hawthorn, a very hard wood, into the soil. The staff took root and a hawthorn bush grew from it. Every Christmas the bush flowers in memory of Jesus' birth.

In 1900 a cutting from the legendary thorn bush at Glastonbury was given to St Albans School in Washington, DC. It first flowered in 1918 and then every Christmas since.

Carols

The word 'carol' comes from the ancient Greek *choros*, which means 'dancing in a circle', and from the Old French word *carole*, meaning 'a song to accompany dancing'.

Originally the carol was not particularly associated with Christmas, and, in fact, was not even a religious song. It may well have started as a song and dance performed at festivals—non-religious celebrations like the coming of spring, midsummer, or harvest time. And it is this association with joyful celebration that links this original carol to our modern Christmas carol.

In early medieval times the Church did not encourage the singing of carols, believing that Christmas should be celebrated in a solemn way. Carols, in any case, were linked to festivals that were a bit too close to the old pagan religions. From about 1400 the Church relaxed its attitude a little, and the fifteenth century saw a great increase in the writing and singing of Christmas carols.

Carols old and new

Probably the oldest carol that we would recognize is 'O Come, O Come Emmanuel'. The words date from the twelfth century. It was originally written in Latin and not translated into English until the first half of the nineteenth century.

There were two great ages of carol writing, in the fifteenth and nineteenth centuries. Many of the older carols were forbidden in England and America by the Puritans in the seventeenth century. It took some time for carols to regain the popularity they had once enjoyed. In fact, it was not until the nineteenth century that the words of many of the older carols were rediscovered, translated, and set to music, to take their place alongside many new carols.

The dates of carols

Two of our favourite carols, 'God Rest Ye Merry Gentlemen' and 'The First Nowell', date from the sixteenth century. So, too, do 'The Twelve Days of Christmas' (originally a counting rhyme for children in France) and 'We Wish You a Merry Christmas', from the English West Country.

Popular eighteenth-century carols include 'The Holly and the Ivy', 'While Shepherds Watched Their Flocks', 'Hark the Herald Angels Sing', and 'O Come All Ye Faithful'.

Among the best-known nineteenth-century carols are 'Silent Night, Holy Night', 'Once in Royal David's City', 'Good King Wenceslas', 'We Three Kings of Orient Are', 'Jingle Bells', 'O Little Town of Bethlehem', 'Away in a Manger' (these last four all originally from America), and 'Ding Dong Merrily on High'.

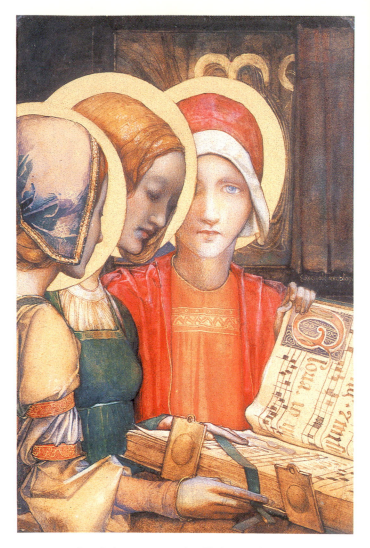

Carols became popular Christmas hymns during the fifteenth century.

Christmas is banned

The Puritans of the seventeenth century believed that an individual's life should be ruled by prayer and stern moral behaviour, both in private and in public. There was no room for frivolity and merrymaking. When they came to power in England they closed the theatres and clamped down on all forms of popular entertainment. Parliament even banned all Christmas festivities in 1644. Soldiers were sent to make sure shops stayed open. Everything possible was done to make Christmas an ordinary working time.

No evergreen plants were to be used as Christmas decoration, and mistletoe, with its pagan Druid associations, was no longer allowed. Even the humble mince pie was banned because it was seen as a temptation to wickedness and over-indulgence!

The main reason the Puritans objected to Christmas was that they thought it had become an excuse for one long party that had lost sight of its religious importance. Although the Puritan attitude may seem mean-spirited, it is worth remembering that there are many people even today who feel that Christmas has strayed some way from its original purpose.

Christmas in America

Events in seventeenth-century England were repeated in what were then the colonies of New England, on the east coast of America. The settlers who arrived in the *Mayflower* were also stern Puritans. In 1659 a law was passed to ban Christmas:

> 'Whosoever shall be found observing any such day as Christmas . . . shall pay five shillings as a fine.'

In the colonies of Virginia, the story was very different. There the settlers were not Puritans, and they had not left England because of religious persecution. So they spent their first Christmas with good food, which probably included wild turkey.

The people fight back

In England, ordinary folk who felt they had been robbed of their traditional holiday by the Puritans voiced their anger. A petition signed by more than 10,000 people from Kent demanded that ' . . . if they could not have their Christmas Day, they would have the king back on his throne.' As events turned out, a Stuart king, Charles II, was restored to the throne in 1660, and the laws passed during the years when the Puritans governed the country were no longer enforced. Yet it was to take some time before Christmas was again celebrated in its former style.

In the Puritan-controlled parts of America, particularly Massachusetts, the ban lasted for twenty-two years. Even then, however, things took a long time to get back to normal. It is amazing to think that not until 1856 did Massachusetts finally agree to make Christmas a legal holiday.

With the restoration of Charles II to the throne of England in 1660, Christmas was restored to its pre-Puritan jollity.

Although Puritans tried to suppress Christmas in America, they were never entirely successful.

JULLIEN'S CELEBRATED POLKAS
No 9.

THE QUEEN & PRINCE ALBERT'S POLKA,
AS PERFORMED FOR THE FIRST TIME BEFORE
HER MOST GRACIOUS MAJESTY,
& HIS ROYAL HIGHNESS PRINCE ALBERT,
ON THE OCCASION OF THEIR VISIT TO
HIS GRACE THE DUKE OF BUCKINGHAM,
AT STOWE &C. &C. &C.

4

THE VICTORIAN CHRISTMAS

A MERRY CHRISTMAS & A HAPPY NEW YEAR
IN LONDON.

A snowy Christmas scene in Victorian London.

◁ Queen Victoria and Prince Albert helped bring back some
of the fun and old traditions of Christmas.

Christmas rediscovered

Christmas was a long and very popular holiday in the Middle Ages. But the effects of the ban that the Puritans placed on celebrations in the seventeenth century, short-lived though it was, somehow seemed difficult to reverse. For various reasons the festival gradually became less important over the next 200 years, almost as if people had forgotten how to enjoy themselves.

This decline in interest certainly had something to do with the way people lived. Formerly, in most parts of Europe, the population had been concentrated mainly in the countryside. Although life for workers on the land was sometimes very harsh and poor, the old traditions of Christmas festivities were deep-rooted. In the industrial towns, on the other hand, the old ways were often left behind in the villages and hamlets from which the new townspeople had come.

Towards the end of the eighteenth century, and even more so in the early nineteenth century, living patterns began to change quite dramatically. With the arrival of railways, people moved in ever greater numbers from the countryside to the new towns and cities to work in the factories. By about 1850 there were probably more people living in towns than in the country, and over twice as many by the end of the century.

The factory owners needed to keep their machines at work for as many days of the year as they could. So there was less time to enjoy the old Christmas

55

'Christmas Out of Doors', New York, 1858.

customs, and the traditional two-week holiday became shorter and shorter. Often it was only Christmas Day itself.

Season of goodwill

In England, where Queen Victoria's long reign lasted from 1837 to 1901, this period is generally called the Victorian age. Some Victorians were unhappy that the old-style Christmas had almost disappeared. Writers such as Charles Dickens in England and Washington Irving in America wrote books about the traditional idea of Christmas and these books became tremendously popular.

Many of the things we most love at Christmas started in the Victorian age, such as the tradition of sending cards and the invention of the cracker. The picture of a fat, jolly Father Christmas (or Santa Claus, as he is called in the United States) dates from Victo-

rian times. The Christmas tree became popular, as did gift shopping in big department stores. In England, the 'Boxing Day' holiday also started in the nineteenth century.

The first Christmas cards

Many children in Victorian England had a special task at Christmas. They had to write greetings to their parents in their very best handwriting. Sometimes adults wrote Christmas letters to each other, but this could take up a great deal of time. The printed Christmas card solved the problem.

The custom of sending printed Christmas cards was started in England by a successful businessman named Sir Henry Cole. Because Sir Henry did not have time to write letters to each of his relatives and many friends, he asked an artist, John Calcott Horsley, to design a Christmas card for him.

The first Christmas card, 1843. It was designed by John Calcott Horsley for Sir Henry Cole.

Horsley's picture showed a happy family eating and drinking, as well as poor people being given food and clothing.

About 1000 of these cards were printed, and those not used by Sir Henry were sold by the printer for one shilling. This was far from cheap at the time, which may be why they did not sell particularly well. Another reason was apparently the choice of picture. It was fine to encourage kindness to the poor, but many people objected to the card because it showed scenes of drinking.

The penny post

One reason why Christmas cards became so popular in the Victorian age was the introduction of the 'penny post'.

In 1840 Sir Rowland Hill suggested a great many changes to the postal service that made it easier and cheaper to send mail. It became possible, for example, to post a letter anywhere in Britain for one penny. Before the introduction of the penny post, the cost depended on the distance the letter had to travel. For

The Royal Mail Van. Improvements in the speed and the lower cost of sending mail helped the Christmas card business to grow tremendously during the nineteenth century.

Why robins?

One reason why the robin became such a popular feature of Christmas cards is that it is an early and welcome visitor to garden bird-tables at the beginning of winter. The fact that the red of its breast was the colour worn by postmen in Victorian Britain was another reason. Red had been chosen because it was considered a royal colour and the Post Office had its origins in the carrying of royal dispatches. Letter boxes in Britain are red for the same reason. Illustrators of Christmas cards in Victorian times were quick to adopt the idea of the robin delivering Christmas mail, like a postman.

In 1861 the postman's red uniform was changed to blue because red showed dirt more easily. By this time, however, the robin had established itself as a firm and lasting favourite.

The first charity Christmas card. It was produced by UNICEF in 1949 from a design by a seven-year-old Czech girl, Jitka Samkova.

A nineteenth-century Christmas card printed by Louis Prang, the 'father' of the
American Christmas card industry.

Posting the Christmas Cards.

With all our best wishes for the Season.

In the last century, 'Post Early for Christmas' meant early on Christmas Eve!

instance, a letter going fifteen miles cost fivepence; twenty miles cost sixpence, and eighty miles one shilling, which was very expensive in those days.

Colour printing

Another reason why more and more people bought and sent Christmas cards was that they soon became easily available as a result of colour printing. New printing machines were invented in the early part of the nineteenth century. They could print in different colours and much faster than the old machines. Now printers could make thousands of cards more quickly and more cheaply.

Some of the new colour printers made playing cards and Valentine Day cards. They quickly took up the idea of Christmas cards as offering a chance to sell more cards than ever before.

The first company to print and sell Christmas cards on a large scale was Charles Goodall & Sons of London in 1862. Scenes that featured snow and robins were popular from the very start.

In 1875, a German printer, Louis Prang, who had settled in New York, having seen how successful Christmas cards were in Britain, started to print them on a new colour press. They were beautifully printed but expensive. A flood of cheap cards entered the country from Germany and, in 1890, Louis Prang—the father of the American Christmas card—went out of business.

Charity Christmas cards

Of all the cards sent at Christmas throughout the world, about one-fifth are from charities such as Oxfam, Save the Children Fund, and similar organizations.

The first charity card was produced in 1949 by the United Nations International Children's Emergency Fund—UNICEF. It was designed by seven-year-old Jitka Samkova of Rudolfo in Czechoslovakia, a town that had been very badly damaged during the Second World War. The people were suffering from shortages of food, medicines and other necessities. In gratitude for the assistance UNICEF gave the town, Jitka painted a picture of children dancing around a maypole which, she explained, 'means joy going round and round'. She used a sheet of glass to work on because there was no paper available.

Jitka's teacher entered her painting in a competition organized by UNICEF. It won first prize and eventually was chosen as the very first UNICEF Christmas card design.

Today UNICEF holds competitions among its 147-country membership and every year a new collection of about 200 designs is chosen. The cards cover all

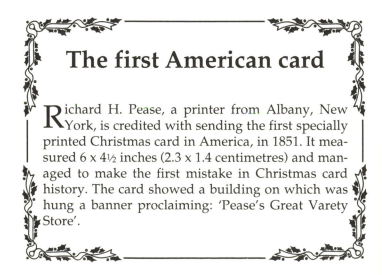

The first American card

Richard H. Pease, a printer from Albany, New York, is credited with sending the first specially printed Christmas card in America, in 1851. It measured 6 x 4½ inches (2.3 x 1.4 centimetres) and managed to make the first mistake in Christmas card history. The card showed a building on which was hung a banner proclaiming: 'Pease's Great Varety Store'.

religions, and non-Christian cards are growing in popularity. Japan, for example, takes about one million UNICEF cards, even though only one per cent of its population is Christian. Throughout the world, some 200 million UNICEF cards are sold every Christmas.

Christmas mail

Until the end of the nineteenth century the British Post Office would deliver Christmas mail on Christmas Day itself. Indeed, when it advised customers to 'post early', it meant early on Christmas Eve. Gradually, however, the massive number of cards involved made it impossible to continue this service. In the United States, nevertheless, it is still possible to have mail delivered on 25 December if it is sent express.

Today the mountain of Christmas mail is staggering. In 1992 about 4000 million pieces will be processed by the US postal services during the three weeks leading up to Christmas Day. In Britain the equivalent figure is about 2000 million.

The great nineteenth-century American illustrator, Thomas Nast, practically invented the modern image of Santa Claus.

Christmas complaints

In America, as early as 1822, the postmaster of Washington DC complained that he had had to add sixteen mailmen at Christmas to deal with cards alone. He wanted the number of cards a person could send limited by law! 'I don't know what we'll do if this keeps on,' he wrote. And this was at a time when only home-made cards were available. When colour printing came in, cards were even bigger business. In 1880, the British magazine *Punch* moaned—with rather better reason—about the 'sleet of Christmas cards'.

London, for example, has a very special way to speed the Chrismas mail to its destination. Under the feet of shoppers runs Mail Rail, a driverless and passengerless train which carries mail—about ten million bags a year—from sorting offices to main-line stations. It runs for twenty-two hours a day, six days a week, taking only thirteen minutes to travel between Paddington and Liverpool Street stations. At Christmas time Mail Rail doubles its length and will carry almost one million cards and letters across London.

Writing to Santa

In some parts of the United States volunteer mailmen dressed as Santa Claus deliver cards and parcels throughout Christmas week.

Many of the largest post offices answer cards sent to Santa Claus, sometimes from less fortunate children or parents for whom Christmas can be a very sad and disappointing time. Many post offices em-

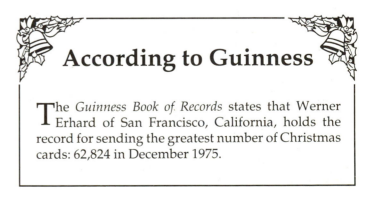

According to Guinness

The *Guinness Book of Records* states that Werner Erhard of San Francisco, California, holds the record for sending the greatest number of Christmas cards: 62,824 in December 1975.

An early letter to Santa

'Dear Mr Santa Claus,
  I only want a pare of skates for Christmas and if it aint cold a sled will do. My old ones bust. If they aint no snow I would like anything you think of. My mamma says you are poor this year . . .'
Printed in the *New York Exchange*, December 1893

ploy volunteer staff who often make sure that these children not only get a reply from Santa but also a gift.

In recent years Santa Claus has received about one million letters from Britain alone! If they are addressed to another country they will be forwarded. Provided they are addressed to Reindeerland SAN TAI, and a return address given, no later than the first week of December, the sender will receive a reply by Christmas Eve.

Charles Dickens: the man who made Christmas

Astonishing as it may seem, by the early part of the nineteenth century Christmas had almost died out. *The Times* newspaper, for example, did not once mention Christmas between 1790 and 1835!

Charles Dickens, with his story *A Christmas Carol*, did more than anyone to change all that. The tale of

Nobody did more than the novelist Charles Dickens to revive the traditional idea of Christmas.

'Scrooge and the Ghost of Christmas Past.' An illustration by Arthur Rackham of an episode from Charles Dickens's *A Christmas Carol.*

Scrooge, the Cratchits, and Tiny Tim was a smash hit from the start.

Dickens wrote *A Christmas Carol* in just two months. He began in early October 1843 and finished at the end of November. After completing it, Dickens wrote delightedly to a friend: 'Charles Dickens wept and laughed and wept again . . . he walked about the black streets of London, fifteen and twenty miles many a night.'

The book was published on 17 December 1843 and immediately sold out. Six thousand copies were sold at five shillings—quite a high price in those days. Dickens declared that 'the book was a most prodigious success—the greatest I think I have ever achieved'. *A Christmas Carol* was so popular that Dickens was asked to read from it in public. His readings from this book and his longer novels drew large audiences in England and America, and Dickens made as much money from them as he did from his writing. However, the strain that these dramatic readings put on him was tremendous and certainly contributed to his death on 9 June 1870.

Hearing of his death, a ragged little girl in London was heard to say, 'Does that mean that Father Christmas is dead?' And although Charles Dickens had not even mentioned Father Christmas in his story, the little girl's remark shows how important to Christmas the famous author had become.

Dickens wrote many other Christmas stories. Perhaps the two best known, other than *A Christmas Carol*, are *The Chimes* and *The Cricket on the Hearth*. There is also a wonderful description of Christmas in *The Pickwick Papers*.

Christmas specialities

There were no turkeys in Europe before about 1520. The Spanish invaders of South America, known as the *conquistadors*, discovered the birds and brought them back to Europe along with tomatoes, potatoes, tobacco, and other local produce.

When turkeys were introduced to Spain from the New World they caused a sensation. Wild turkeys could grow to 50–60 pounds (22–27 kilograms), which made Europe's largest bird, the great bustard, at about 33 pounds (15 kilograms), look a bit puny. Turkeys were brought to Britain around 1549.

Because they were easy to raise and quickly put on weight, these birds became very popular and were even the farmers' own choice for Christmas. Yet not everyone liked them. Charles Estienne, a Frenchman, wrote of them in 1564:

> 'This bird is a bin of oats . . . from which no other pleasure can be derived than noise and fury . . . The flesh is delicate but tasteless and hard to digest . . . These Indian hens eat as much as mules.'

Turkeys in boots

Before there were suitable road and rail links between town and country, turkeys had to be walked to market. In England, Norfolk was, and still is, one of the centres of turkey breeding, and, as Christmas approached, the birds were assembled for the journey to London. The turkeys' feet were protected from the

'A bin of oats . . . from which no other pleasure can be derived than noise and fury' is how a Frenchman described the turkey in 1564.

frozen mud with 'boots' made from old sacking or even leather. Geese, however, did not take to boots, presumably because they could not easily be fitted

Turkey farming

In Europe, where there are no wild turkeys, domesticated turkeys have to be bred on farms. In America, wild turkeys were at first bred only for their feathers. The turkey-feather duster was invented by William Hoag in Iowa in 1872, and the company he founded lasted for more than 100 years.

Today most turkeys are either Broad-breasted Bronzes or Beltsville Small Whites. It takes about nine months for them to reach their top weight of about 36 pounds (16 kilograms). Older turkeys tend to be tough and useless for cooking.

A nineteenth-century illustration of a turkey complete with Father Christmas face and a chain of office made from sausages.

Wild turkeys

The first European settlers in North America found plenty of wild turkeys. By 1737 a 40-pound (18-kilogram) wild turkey from Virginia cost 30 cents. In Kentucky, around the same date, such birds were much cheaper than farm-raised chickens.

Wild turkeys can still be found from Pennsylvania to Florida and westward to Colorado and Arizona. They are also native to most of Mexico. They are much smaller and leaner than the huge farm-raised birds, growing, on average, to 13 pounds (6 kilograms).

Changing tastes

Americans, like Europeans, nowadays roast their Christmas turkey. But at the time of the Revolution,

over webbed feet! So their feet had to be covered in a protective coating of tar. The distance from Norfolk to London is about 100 miles, and the trek would have taken at least a week.

An American cartoon of the nineteenth century, showing the progress of a turkey from farm to Christmas table.

The Victorian illustrator Kate Greenaway's view of the well-stocked Christmas table, including a lovely Twelfth Night cake.

According to Guinness

The *Guinness Book of Records* says that the heaviest turkey ever recorded weighed 78 pounds 14 ounces (35.8 kilograms) without its feathers! It won the annual 'heaviest turkey competition' in London on 15 December 1982.

Americans preferred to cook it differently, as one old ditty explained:

> 'Turkey boiled is turkey spoiled
> And turkey roast is turkey lost.
> But for turkey braised
> The Lord be praised.'

Braising is a way of slowly cooking meat in a kind of stew which includes vegetables.

In the nineteenth century, both in America and Britain, only the white meat from the breast was considered good enough for guests. The dark meat of the legs would only have been eaten by the family on the days after Christmas. Or it would have been given to the servants.

The typical turkey stuffing of Victorian times was rich and spicy. It contained oysters, chestnuts, saffron, prunes, cinnamon, port wine, oranges, cloves, and anchovies. A string of sausages, like a chain of office, was often hung around the turkey's neck.

Christmas pudding comes from the spiced porridge known as frumenty. Its presentation in the meal is a very dramatic moment.

The Twelfth Night cake

The old-fashioned Twelfth Night cake was close to what we would call a Christmas cake. Sometimes these cakes were of spectacular size, such as this one advertised in 1811:

> 'Extraordinary Large Twelfth Cake, eighteen feet in circumference, to be seen at Adams's, 41 Cheapside, opposite Wood Street. The cake considerably surpasses in size any that has been made in London, or, in fact, in the world: its weight is nearly half a ton, and actually contains nearly two hundred and a halfweight of currants, and upwards of ONE THOUSAND EGGS. This wonderful Cake is ready for public inspection.'

Mince pies

Mince pies became popular in the Victorian age, but their history, too, is a long one. In the twelfth century, as has been mentioned, knights returning from the Crusades in the Holy Land introduced to Europe many Middle Eastern ways of cooking. Some of these dishes mixed sweet tastes with savoury, and recipes of meat cooked with fruit and sweet spices were popular.

In Elizabethan times mince pies were still a mixture of meat and fruit. They were called 'shrid' pies because they contained shredded meat and suet,

which is the hard fat found around the kidneys of cows or sheep. The meat and suet were mixed with dried fruit such as raisins and currants. It was traditional to add three spices—cinnamon, cloves and nutmeg—which stood for the three gifts given to Jesus by the Wise Men.

The mixture was then baked in a pastry case, not a round one like the mince pies of today, but oblong to represent Jesus' crib. To complete the pie, a little pastry baby often decorated the lid.

The Puritans tried to ban mince pies. 'Such a pye,' they said, 'is an hodge-podge of superstition, Popery, the devil, and all its works.'

It was once thought lucky to eat a mince pie on each of the twelve days of Christmas. Each pie would be eaten in a different house in order to bring good luck to the household and the eater for the next twelve months.

Plum pudding

> '. . . When the roast beef has been removed, when the pudding in all the glory of its splendour shines upon the table . . . How beautifully it steams! How delicious it smells! How round it is! A kiss is round, the horizon is round, the earth is round, the moon is round . . . So is plum pudding.'

The Illustrated London News 1848

As we have seen, our traditional Christmas pudding goes back to the spiced porridge known in the Middle Ages as frumenty. In fact, it was often called 'plum pottage', meaning a mixture as thick as porridge. Later it was sometimes called a 'hackin' pudding' because the ingredients were chopped or 'hacked' before going into the pudding.

After that it became the familiar 'plum' pudding, although in the nineteenth century, instead of fresh plums, it only contained prunes, which are dried plums. Gradually the prunes gave way to other dried fruit, especially currants, sultanas and raisins.

'Stir-Up Sunday'

According to a very old tradition, everyone in the family had to help stir the Christmas pudding mixture. This was thought to bring good health and luck to each member of the family in the coming year. The day reserved for this operation was 'Stir-Up Sunday', the fifth Sunday before Christmas, the reason being that in the prayer book for this Sunday of the year, it says, 'Stir up, we beseech Thee, O Lord, the will of thy faithful people.'

An old recipe for Christmas pudding

This is what went into the Christmas pudding prepared for King George I in 1714:

> 1 lb (500 g) eggs
> 1½ lb (750 g) shredded suet
> 1 lb (500 g) each of: dried plums (prunes),
>   raisins, sultanas, mixed orange and lemon
>   peel, currants, flour, sugar, breadcrumbs
> 1 teaspoon mixed spices (cinnamon, cloves)
> 1 teaspoon grated nutmeg
> ½ pint (250 ml) milk
> ½ teaspoon salt
> Juice of one lemon
> Glass of brandy

The mixture was wrapped in a cloth and boiled for eight hours. On Christmas Day it was then boiled again for another two hours. It served about thirty people.

Little Jack Horner: a true story?

'Little Jack Horner
Sat in a corner
Eating his Christmas pie:
He put in a thumb,
And pulled out a plum,
And said "What a good boy am I".'

Jack Horner was said to have been chief steward to the abbot of Glastonbury in Somerset during the early sixteenth century. The abbot was worried that King Henry VIII was going to pull down the abbey. To prevent this, the wily old abbot thought he might try to bribe the king with the gift of some lands the abbey owned. So he ordered a great pie to be baked and in it he put the deeds to twelve of the manors of Glastonbury.

Jack Horner was sent off to the king with the pie. But when the king received his unusual gift, there were only eleven deeds inside. No wonder Jack Horner was pleased with himself. He had indeed pulled out a nice 'plum'.

Little Jack Horner—was he a real person?

≺ A Christmas dinner at sea, 1889.

'Hurrah for the Pudding!' 1870.

The charmed pudding

Now that so many puddings come ready-made from supermarkets, we have almost lost one of the oldest and nicest of Christmas traditions.

When Christmas puddings were made at home, silver charms and new coins were put into the mixture. Whoever found the charm in their piece of pudding would have good luck in the year to come.

The tradition, as we have seen, dates right back to ancient Rome and the Saturnalia feast, when it was the custom to place a dried bean inside a cake. Whoever found the bean was 'king' for the evening, permitted to order the other guests to make complete fools of themselves. This tradition continued with the Twelfth Night cake on 6 January, and lasted until almost the end of the Victorian age.

Rich and poor

Christmas in Victorian times could be the best of times, but it could also be the worst. Those with enough money could afford to celebrate in style. On a salary, say, of £200 a year, a family could live very well. But many people earned less than half that, in which case life could be hard. And perhaps one-third of the population lived in poverty. For most, meat was a luxury. Best meat cost ninepence a pound, rabbits one shilling each. An unskilled worker might earn twenty-five shillings a week (there were twelve pennies in a shilling and twenty shillings in a pound), so meat seldom appeared on the family plates at dinner time.

A nice fat goose cost about five shillings. For many people this would have been their pay for a day. A domestic servant 'below stairs' earned as little as £12 a year, so that a goose would have cost her ten days' wages. Yet somehow Christmas could be made special, even if it meant only an orange and a farthing (a quarter of a penny) in the stocking, or the once-a-year treat of eating goose or beef.

Shopping for Christmas

There were no refrigerators in Victorian homes. Wealthy families might have an ice-house, but for most people there was no way of keeping food fresh for any length of time. Many lived in overcrowded conditions anyway and had no room to store food. So they were obliged to shop from day to day, and to buy as cheaply as they could.

The best day for shopping was Christmas Eve; and the best place to go was the street market, full of noise and activity, and on Christmas Eve particularly excit-

---

According to Guinness

The largest Christmas pudding recorded in the *Guinness Book of Records* weighed 3064 pounds (1390 kilograms)! A company named Herbert Adams of Victoria, Australia, made it in 1987, and it took about three weeks to prepare the ingredients.

The ceremonial entry of the Christmas pudding 'below stairs'.

ing. People who left the shopping as late as possible might be able to get a goose that little bit cheaper or pick up some bruised fruit or vegetables for a few pennies.

The street market

Here is a description of a typical Victorian street market by Henry Mayhew in his *London Labour and London Poor*, published in 1851:

> '. . . The crowd is almost impassable. Indeed the scene in these parts has more of the character of a fair than a market. There are hundreds of stalls, and every stall has one or two lights. Either it is illuminated by the intense white light of the new gas lamp, or else it is brightened up by the red smoky flame of the old-fashioned grease lamp . . .
>
> 'Some stalls are crimson with the fire shining through the holes beneath the baked chestnut stove . . .
>
> 'The crisp Christmas air is filled with the calls of the stall-holders: "Chestnuts all 'ot, a penny a score [twenty]," bawls one. "Fine warrnuts [walnuts], sixteen a penny, fine warrnuts," shouts another. "Now's your time! Beautiful whelks, a penny a lot!" invites yet another.'

Christmas at the Cratchits

This is how Charles Dickens described a poor family's dinner in *A Christmas Carol*. The Cratchits had taken their goose to the local baker to have it cooked. Now they were ready to enjoy the best meal of the year:

> 'Such a bustle ensued that you might have thought a goose the rarest of all birds . . . Mrs Cratchit made the gravy (ready beforehand in a saucepan) hissing hot; Master Peter mashed the potatoes with incredible vigour; Miss Belinda sweetened up the apple-sauce; Martha

Christmas shopping in a Danish street market, 1867.

dusted the hot plates . . . the two young Cratchits set chairs for everybody, not forgetting themselves, and mounting guard upon their posts, crammed spoons into their mouths, lest they should shriek for goose before their turn came to be helped. At last the dishes were set on and grace was said . . .

'There never was such a goose . . . Its tenderness and flavour, size and cheapness were the themes of universal admiration. Eked out by apple-sauce and mashed potatoes, it was a sufficient dinner for the whole family; indeed, as Mrs Cratchit said with great delight (surveying one small atom of bone upon the dish), they hadn't ate it all at last! Yet every one had had enough, and the youngest Cratchits in particular were steeped in sage and onion to the eyebrows! . . . Mrs Cratchit left the room alone—too nervous to bear witness—to take the pudding up, and bring it in.

'Suppose it should not be done enough! Suppose it should break in turning out! Suppose somebody should have got over the wall of the back-yard, and stolen it, while they were merry with the goose . . .

'Hallo! A great deal of steam! The pudding was out of the copper [a large metal tank used for boiling clothes, and usually kept out in the back-yard]. A smell like washing day! That was the cloth [in which the pudding was wrapped]. A smell like an eating-house and a pastrycook's next door to each other . . . That was the pudding! In half a minute Mrs Cratchit entered:

Saving for Christmas

Many Victorian families of modest means put money into a Christmas club, sometimes called the 'Goose Club'. During the months leading up to Christmas, the mother of the family would put by a few pennies here, sixpence there, until she had saved enough to buy some Christmas treats—a goose or piece of beef for the main course, and perhaps some oranges, nuts and a few sweets for the children's stockings.

There was almost always a Christmas raffle at the club. With luck you might even win a goose or a bottle of rum or cheap brandy.

flushed, but smiling proudly—with the pudding, like a speckled cannon-ball, so hard and firm, blazing in half of half a quartern of ignited brandy . . . with Christmas holly stuck into the top.'

Slim pickings

If life in the Victorian town or city was tough, it was often harder still in the country. The average wage for a farm worker was eight shillings a week, less than a quarter of what an unskilled city worker earned.

The usual diet for many farm labourers and their families consisted of a dish called 'kettlebroth', which was made of bread dissolved in hot water, with a little salt and milk added. Sometimes there was pudding made of flour, salt, suet and water. It was served with whatever vegetables could be had, and occasionally a bit of bacon.

For centuries farm labourers had been allowed to catch rabbits and other wild game, but laws had now

'Boys Rabbiting', by the Victorian artist Sir John Everett Millais. Rabbits were an important addition to the diets of the poor and would have featured in many a Christmas meal.

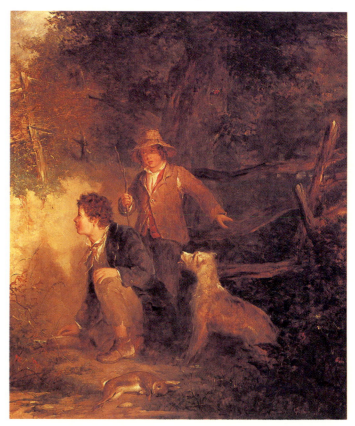

been passed to stop this ancient right. Up to 1857, if he broke these laws, an offender could be sent as a convict to Australia for seven years!

At Christmas time there might be a nice piece of smoked bacon saved from the autumn, traditionally the time of year when pigs were killed and their meat preserved, as in centuries past, by pickling it with spices or in salted water, or by smoking it over a wood fire. Alternatively, there might be a fine pie in which were baked a few rabbits or a pheasant poached at great risk from the squire's woodland. In some counties the lady of the manor would visit each family on the squire's land with gifts of cheese and meat or warm woollen clothes for the children.

It was considered a Christian duty for the wealthy to distribute Christmas gifts to the local poor, old, and infirm.

A French illustration of 1858 shows an 'upstairs/downstairs' Christmas.

'Above stairs'

At the opposite end of the social scale, life in the Victorian age afforded many comforts and luxuries. A typical Christmas dinner in a well-off household might well have included:

Vegetable soup
Oyster patties
Roast turkey or goose
Boiled leg of mutton with caper sauce
Jelly made of port wine
Mince pies
Plum pudding

A right royal feast

In 1840 Queen Victoria entertained eighteen guests for Christmas dinner at Windsor Castle. They were served:

Turtle soup
Haddock or sole
Beef or roast swan
Veal, chicken, partridge or curried rabbit
Pheasant or capon of chicken
Mince pies

In addition to the dinner there was also a sideboard on which sat a boar's head, sausages, brawn, lark and pheasant pie, a joint of roast beef, a roast mutton and a roast turkey. Just in case you were still peckish after the meal.

In 1851 the roast swan was dropped from the Christmas menu.

Apples and candles were favourite tree decorations in nineteenth-century Scandinavia.

A pie from the Queen

For centuries royal and noble families were expected to give Christmas gifts to household servants and workers on the estates. Queen Victoria was no exception. Employees on her estates were given a shoulder of lamb, but the more important staff and friends would receive a very special pie.

Queen Victoria's Christmas pies involved an enormous amount of work. Each pie would contain a variety of birds, all of which had first had their bones removed. The first was a woodcock, small enough to put inside a pheasant, which in turn was placed inside a chicken. The chicken was then stuffed into a turkey. Finally the turkey was packed around with stuffing and baked in a rich pastry. When the pie was cut, every slice had the distinctive flavour of each of the four birds.

The Christmas tree

Trees have played an important part in religion for thousands of years. The oak, for example, was sacred to the ancient Greek god Zeus as it was to the Druids of northern Europe. In ancient Rome evergreen trees were thought to have special powers and were used for decoration. In pagan Scandinavia fir trees and ash trees were often hung with war and hunting trophies to bring good luck; and as Christianity took over from the old pagan religions, it, too, made use of fir trees in certain ceremonies, not only at Christmas but also during Easter and at midsummer. The maypole, for example, was probably originally a pagan fir tree.

In the Middle Ages the Church decorated trees with apples on Christmas Eve, which was known then as Adam and Eve's Day as a reminder of the apple Adam had eaten from the Tree of Knowledge in the Garden of Eden. Adam was supposed to have brought with him a cutting of this tree when he and Eve were driven out of the Garden.

A German tradition

The Christmas tree tradition seems to have started in Germany. In the sixteenth century, city merchants would carry a fir tree decorated with paper flowers through the streets on Christmas Eve. A great feast was held in the market square, followed by dancing around the Christmas tree, and finally the tree was ceremonially burned.

By that time Christmas trees had become very popular in Alsace, which was then part of Germany. In fact, they were a little too popular. The town

Dancing around a Christmas tree in Moscow during the darkest days of the Second World War.

The Christmas tree
became universally
popular during the
Victorian era.

council of Ammerschwir, worried that too many fir trees were being cut down, gave an order that nobody 'shall have for Christmas more than one bush of more than eight shoes' length' (about 4 feet or 1.3 metres high).

Early trees

During the seventeenth and eighteenth centuries Christmas trees or *Christbaumen* appeared in different forms. Sometimes only the tips of fir branches were used, often hung upside down, especially over doorways. Some people took fir branches and fixed them to wooden pyramids which were then decorated, usually with paper roses, nuts, and apples.

It was also traditional to have a kind of triangular candle-holder called the *lichtstock*, which reminds us of the *menorah*, the eight-branched candle-holder used during the Jewish holiday of Hanukkah.

Christmas trees were from the start more popular in the countries of northern Europe than in the lands further south. One reason, of course, was that there are more fir trees in the northern forests. Another is that Germany, England, and other northern countries had become Protestant during the sixteenth century. Southern countries such as France, Spain, and Italy were Catholic. Not warming to the idea of the 'Protestant' tree, they adopted the crib, or *crèche*, as the centrepiece of their Christmas decoration.

A Hanover childhood

Liselotte von der Palz, a German noblewoman who became Duchess of Orléans in France, wrote in 1708 about her childhood memories of Christmas in Hanover about fifty years earlier. This is how she remembered it:

> 'Tables are fixed up like altars and outfitted for each child with all sorts of things such as clothes, silver, dolls, sugar sticks and so forth. Boxwood trees were set on the tables, and a candle was fastened to each branch.'

The Christmas tree comes to Britain

The eighteenth-century kings of England were of German origin, from Hanover, and perhaps it was they who introduced the *Christbaum* tradition to England, although there is no written evidence.

During the nineteenth century the fashion was for smaller trees on a table rather than on the floor.

The earliest record of a Christmas tree in England dates from 1800. Dr John Watkins, a visitor to Queen's Lodge at Windsor, described the tree that belonged to Queen Charlotte, the wife of George III:

> 'In the middle of the room stood an immense tub with a yew tree placed in it, from the branches hung bunches of sweetmeats [sweets], almonds, and raisins in papers, fruits and toys, most tastefully arranged, and the whole illuminated by small wax candles.
>
> 'After the company had walked round and admired the tree, each child obtained a portion of the sweets it bore, together with a toy, and then all returned home quite delighted.'

Prince Albert shows the way

The member of the royal family who really made the Christmas tree popular in England was the Prince Consort, Albert of Saxe-Coburg, the German husband of Queen Victoria. In 1848 *The Illustrated London News* printed a full-page illustration of the royal

Christmas tree at Windsor. The fashion quickly spread.

Charles Dickens, too, described the 'new' Christmas trees in 1850:

> 'I have been looking on this evening at a merry company of children assembled round that pretty German toy, a Christmas tree. The tree was planted in the middle of a great round table, and towered high above their heads. It was brilliantly lighted by a multitude of little tapers; and everywhere sparkled and glittered with bright objects. There were rosy-cheeked dolls, hiding behind green leaves . . . there were jolly-faced little men, far more agreeable in appearance than many real men—and no wonder, for their heads came off and showed them to be full of sugar plums . . . As a pretty girl before delightedly whispered to another pretty girl, "There was everything—and more!" '

Norway's gift to Britain

The great Christmas tree that stands each year in London's Trafalgar Square comes from Norway as a gift from the people of Oslo to the City of Westminster. The tradition began in 1947 as an expression of goodwill and gratitude for Britain's help to Norway during the Second World War. In return, the City of Westminster presented a rose garden to the people of Oslo in 1972.

The Trafalgar Square tree is a Norwegian spruce usually about 70 feet (21 metres) high, though the

Queen Victoria's husband, Prince Albert (far right) did a great deal to popularize the Christmas tree.

The Christmas tree in London's Trafalgar Square has been a gift from the people of Norway since 1947.

The legend of St Boniface

An old legend claims that in the early eighth century St Boniface was sent from England to bring Christianity to the Druids in Germany. In order to demonstrate to the Druids that their oak tree was not sacred, the saint chopped down a large oak. As it came crashing to the ground, it smashed all the surrounding trees, except one—a little fir. St Boniface saw his opportunity and, pointing to the fir, remarked, 'Let this tree be called the tree of the Christ Child.' Indeed, in Germany, a Christmas tree is still referred to as the *Christbaum*, or 'Christ's tree'.

Victorian children decorating their tree.

estants from Germany. One of the towns they founded was Bethlehem, Pennsylvania. And it was from that neighbourhood that we have the earliest mention of a Christmas tree in America. In his diary for 20 December 1820, Matthew Zahn wrote: 'Sally and our Thomas and William Hensel was out for Christmas trees on the hill . . .'

The Rockefeller Center Christmas tree

America has celebrated Christmas around the tree at Rockefeller Center, New York, since 1931. That Christmas was spent under the dark shadow cast by the Great Depression. Construction workers on the muddy building site placed the little tree among the dirt and rubble and queued up alongside it to receive their wages.

The first formal Christmas tree in the completed Rockefeller Center was put up for the 1933 season, in front of the then new seventy-storey RCA Building.

In 1941, two live reindeer were borrowed from Bronx Zoo and were housed in cages on either side of the Prometheus Fountain. That was also the year of the Japanese attack on the American fleet at Pearl Harbor, and during the war years the tree had no lights. In 1945, however, with the war over, the tree was trimmed with fluorescent plastic globes that glowed when a 'black' light was focused on them.

In 1964 the lighting ceremony became an annual television event watched across the whole nation. In addition, about 2,500,000 people visit the Rockefeller Center during the Christmas holidays to see the magnificent tree. Most of the trees used are Norway or white spruce, with the occasional balsam fir. On av-

tallest, put up in 1975, measured just over 85 feet (26 metres). It is cut in late November and presented to the Lord Mayor of London, who goes to Oslo to receive it. The tree is then shipped to Felixstowe and taken to London by road on the back of a huge transporter. Once there, it is erected and dressed with over 500 white lights.

The American experience

During the American War of Independence there were German troops, Hessians, fighting on the British side. It is likely that they brought the tradition of the Christmas fir tree with them.

Many of those who settled in Pennsylvania in the eighteenth and early nineteenth centuries were Prot-

America's national Christmas tree

The massive sequoia known as the 'General Grant Tree' is in King's Canyon National Park, California. It stands over 267 feet (90 metres) high and is about 4000 years old, which means it was already ancient when Jesus was born. It was made the official national Christmas tree of America in 1925, and every year a Christmas service is held at its base.

The first Christmas tree at the Rockefeller Center in New York was erected in 1931 and had 700 bulbs. Now there are over 25,000.

Practical tips

A Christmas tree must have plenty of water. A 6-foot (2-metre) tree can drink 6-7 pints of water a day. First cut off about 1 inch (2.5 centimetres) from the bottom of the trunk. Put the tree in a bucket of water and keep it outside for a couple of days. When you bring the tree indoors, try to keep it in a stand that will hold water and make sure there is plenty of water in it every day. This will prevent the tree dying too quickly.

If a Christmas tree dries out, it can catch fire more easily. Fir and pine trees are full of a kind of juice called resin, and once alight they will burn quickly and fiercely. Keep a fire extinguisher or a bucket of water handy. Do not use live candles as decoration. Make sure your electric tree lights are in good order, and never leave these lights on overnight or when the house is empty. Do not place the tree near an open fire or any heater that might cause it to catch alight.

erage they are 70 feet (21 metres) but the tallest, in 1950 and 1952, stood at 85 feet (26 metres).

The first tree in 1933 sparkled with 700 bulbs. In 1991 five miles of wire was used for the 25,300 bulbs decorating the tree.

According to Guinness

The world's tallest cut Christmas tree, according to the *Guinness Book of Records*, was put up at the Northgate Shopping Centre, Seattle, Washington in December 1950. It was a Douglas fir and stood 221 feet (67 metres) tall. The tallest tree ever measured was also a Douglas fir. When measured in 1902, in Canada, it stood 415 feet (126.5 metres) high.

Buying a Christmas tree

The fresher a tree is, the better and safer it will be. Here are a few things to look for before you buy:

- Needles should be a nice shiny green. They should not be browned or mottled green. Needles should not be able to be pulled off easily. If a lot of needles fall off when the tree is moved, the tree is already dead.
- Branches should be able to be bent easily without snapping off.
- The trunk should be a little sticky with sap.

Christmas tree decorations

When the Christmas tree was first accepted as part of the seasonal festivities, the most popular decorations were home-made, usually consisting of paper flowers or apples, biscuits, and sweets. The earliest decorations to be bought rather than made at home came from Germany, and particularly from the city of Nuremburg. This city was, and still is, famous for the manufacture of toys. Since the end of the eighteenth century it had been known especially for its tin toys, and these included model soldiers, stars, crosses, and flowers for the Christmas tree.

At about the same time, German manufacturers also started making wax decorations, usually of the baby Jesus or of angels. Many were sold abroad, particularly in the United States where large numbers of German immigrants lived.

Lauscha: birthplace of glass ornaments

The little town of Lauscha is in the forest of Thuringia in Germany and since about 1590 has had one industry—glass-blowing. In 1848 'six dozen of Christmas tree ornaments in three sizes' were made. In 1867 the town got a gasworks. This changed everything. Previously the glass-blowers had to use charcoal fires which produced a varying intensity of heat that made work difficult. Now they had a steady supply of even-burning flame.

The making of glass ornaments was originally a home industry in which every member of the family took part. First the glass-blower himself heated one end of a hollow glass rod over a flame. He blew into the tube until a bubble of glass started to form at the melted end. The bubble was put into the bottom half of a mould and the top half was pressed down on to the glass. Now the bubble was completely encased in the mould. The molten glass filled the mould and took on its shape, which might be a *Weinachtsmann* (Santa Claus), a dog, a cat, a piece of fruit, or any of up to 5000 different designs!

By the time the ornament was taken out of the mould, it had hardened. Now it was given to a child in the family who cut off the 'spike' of glass that had attached the ornament to its glass rod.

The glass-blower's wife now took over. She filled the ornament about a quarter full with a silver liquid.

Buying a Christmas tree on the streets of New York. The first Christmas tree business was started in America in 1851. Now over 40 million are sold in the USA each year.

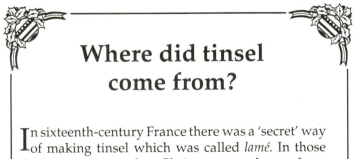

Where did tinsel come from?

In sixteenth-century France there was a 'secret' way of making tinsel which was called *lamé*. In those days it was not used on Christmas trees but as decoration on soldiers' uniforms. *Lamé* was made by pulling copper wire through very small holes until the wire became as fine as human hair. It was then flattened by heavy rollers. Despite every attempt by French *lamé*-makers to preserve their secret, it soon leaked out to Germany, where it was used as the Christmas tree decoration we know as tinsel.

Old hand-blown Christmas tree ornaments are now collectors' items.

Quickly she would swirl the liquid around to cover the inside of the ornament. This made the glass look like a mirror.

The next morning the ornament was dipped in a special paint called lacquer. The lacquer smelled strongly, a bit like glue, and it was said you could smell a glass-blower's house from quite a distance. The glass-blowers themselves did not notice it, however, because they had become used to the smell.

Woolworth steps in

Around 1880 America discovered Lauscha. F.W. Woolworth, the founder of Woolworth stores, went to Lauscha and bought a few glass Christmas tree ornaments, not believing that such objects would sell in any great quantity. Within a day he had sold out. Next year he bought more, and within a week they, too, had gone. The year after that he bought 200,000 Lauscha ornaments.

During the First World War supplies of ornaments from Lauscha to Britain and America ceased. American manufacturers began to make their own Christmas tree ornaments. They developed new techniques and were eventually able to turn out as many ornaments in a single minute as could be made in a whole day at Lauscha.

There are hardly any glass-blowers left in Lauscha today who remember the traditional methods of making glass ornaments. Those objects that were made in the old days are now worth a lot of money because they are collected as antiques.

The first candles

The earliest lights on Christmas trees were candles or 'tapers'. Because beeswax was so expensive, these candles were made of tallow, which comes from animal fat, usually sheep, that has been melted down and allowed to harden. When tallow burns, it splut-

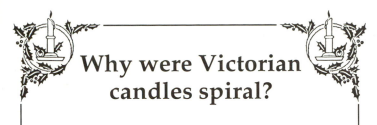

Why were Victorian candles spiral?

This is simply a practical matter. As the wax near the flame melts, it drips down the sides of the candle. With a smooth-sided candle, if it is leaning slightly, the wax runs down on to the floor. With a spiral candle, it does not matter if the candle is tilting a little because the wax will run down through the grooves without dripping.

ters, making quite a lot of smoke, and it has a distinctly sheepish smell!

There is a legend that Martin Luther, the founder of the Protestant Church in Germany in the sixteenth century, was the first person to put candles on a Christmas tree. Luther was walking home one winter evening, deep in thought. He looked up, saw the stars twinkling through the branches of the fir trees, and was so inspired by the sight that when he arrived home he set up a tree and decorated it with candles.

Fire risks

None of the early candles were particularly safe. And with some nineteenth-century magazines recommending to their readers that a 12-foot (3-metre) tree should have no less than 400 candles, it is hardly surprising that Christmas tree fires were a real danger. One American newspaper report dated 25 December 1887 described a fire in Matawan, New Jersey:

'Until this evening Christmas was a joyous one in the home of Mr Robert Morris . . . Shortly before six this evening Mrs Morris decided to light the candles of her Christmas tree, which stood in the front room. Frank Morris, her six-year-old son, was close beside her as she with matches touched one candle then another. Frank became over-anxious, and seizing hold a branch of the Christmas tree to see whether one

Legend has it that Martin Luther (seen here with his family) was the first to decorate a tree with candles.

of the candles was lighting, he upset the tree. In an instant the whole tree was on fire. The tree in falling set fire to the house, and also to the clothing of Frank. When it was discovered that Frank's clothing was ablaze an attempt was made to put out the fire on him. It was too late, however . . . The house, a little frame structure, was also burned down, causing a loss of about $500.'

It is amazing that there were not more tragedies such as this. The risk was probably lessened by the fact that trees were usually cut only on Christmas Eve, so that they were fresher and less likely to ignite. Also, people knew the possible danger and customarily kept a bucket of water close to hand.

One safety measure was the invention by the American, Charles Kirchhof, in December 1867, of a candle-holder with a weight on the bottom to help the candle stand upright. The problem was that the weight often caused the candle to slide off the branch.

In 1879 another American, Frederick Artz, invented a candle-holder with a spring clip that could

A modern artificial Christmas tree makes up in convenience what it lacks in charm.

be attached to the branch. Made of tin, with a little cup at the bottom to catch melted wax, this type of holder became a great success and can still be bought today.

Enter electricity

The American Thomas Edison invented the electric light bulb in 1879. Three years later, Edward H. Johnson, who worked for Edison's company, had Christmas tree bulbs especially made for himself at the factory. Mr Johnson proudly displayed the first ever *electric* Christmas tree lights at his home on Fifth Avenue, New York City. They caused a sensation, as this description by a local newspaper reporter indicates:

> 'There was a large Christmas tree . . . It was brilliantly lighted with many colored globes about as large as an English walnut and was turning some six times a minute on a little pine box. There were eighty lights in all encased in these dainty glass eggs, and about equally divided between red, white and blue. As the tree turned, the colors alternated, all the lamps going out and being relit at every revolution.
> 'I need not tell you that the evergreen was a pretty sight—one can hardly imagine anything prettier . . . the fantastic tree itself with its starry fruit was kept going by the slight electric current brought from the main office on a filmy wire. The tree was kept revolving by a little hidden crank below the floor which was turned by electricity. It was a superb exhibition.'

As each light had to be hand-made, such a set as Mr Johnson's was far too expensive for ordinary families. Some years were to pass before mass-manufactured Christmas tree lights were widely available.

Smaller and better

In 1903 the Ever-Ready Company of New York began to make 'strings' of lights which it called 'festoons'. Each string had twenty-eight bulbs which cost $28, about a week's wages for an average family at the time.

The bulbs at first used for Christmas tree lights were large, and a further disadvantage was that if one bulb went out, so did the whole lot. And as it was not obvious which bulb had failed, every one had to be checked.

In 1927 the General Electric Company of America introduced tiny bulbs that would not get too hot. The company also changed the way the electricity reached the bulbs, so that if one bulb went out, the others stayed on. Now it was easy to see which bulb needed replacing.

The Christmas crib

A crib was originally a box that held straw or hay on which cattle fed. The Bible story also uses the old word 'manger' (from the French verb, spelt the same but pronounced differently, meaning 'to eat'). Today, however, the Christmas crib, or *crèche*, represents the whole scene in the stable where Jesus was born. In addition to the crib or manger where Jesus sleeps, we see Mary and Joseph, oxen and asses, shepherds, angels, and the three Wise Men.

Perhaps the earliest Christmas crib was the one used by Pope Sixtus III around the year 400. The Pope introduced the tradition of midnight mass on Christmas Eve in Rome, and in the church of Santa Maria Maggiore he built a copy of Jesus' crib.

Centuries later, St Francis made the crib even more popular. In 1223, while staying in the Italian village of Greccio, quite close to his home town of Assisi, St Francis told a good friend, Giovanni Velitta, that he wanted to bring to life the story of Jesus' birth.

Giovanni promptly built a realistic copy of the Nativity stable complete with live animals and real people dressed up as Mary and Joseph, the shepherds, the magi and the angels. The crib, or *presepio*, caused a sensation, and was so successful that St Francis received permission from the Pope to re-create the Nativity scene each year. Later, the live animals and people were replaced by models, although in some churches these models were life-sized.

The art of the crib

In the eighteenth century the making of Christmas cribs was taken very seriously, and nowhere more so than at Naples in Italy. The finest sculptors and painters were employed to make the figures and animals. Craftsmen in wood carved hands and feet. The little

A child makes an offering of Christmas goodies to the family's Christmas *crèche* or crib.

models of people were dressed in beautiful miniature clothes—rare silks and satins, cuffs and collars edged with fine lace, tiny buttons, ear-rings, and necklaces. The animals, too, were made by specialists. Every effort was made to render the scene as lifelike as possible by introducing all the local characters one would have seen in the Italian town and countryside at that time. Sometimes there were hundreds of human and animal figures, all exquisitely carved and decorated.

Santons

In Provence, in southern France, there is a variation of the Italian *presepio* called the *santon*. On the first Sunday of December a *Foire des Santons* is held in the Mediterranean port of Marseilles. At this fair dozens of booths are lined up along one of the city's main streets, each selling the little painted clay figures for the Christmas *crèche*. Apart from the traditional figures of the infant Jesus, Mary, and Joseph and so on, there are also local country characters such as the village idiot. Every year families buy a couple of new figures to add to their *crèche*.

One of the most famous of these old Neapolitan cribs can be seen every Christmas at the Metropolitan Museum of Art in New York. Under a magnificent Christmas tree the Nativity scene spreads out, while from the branches a host of angels looks down on the busy activity below.

Christmas music

The word 'wait' comes from *waitier*, an old French word meaning 'to watch'. The waits were originally the town's watchmen, what we would call security guards. They were paid by the town council to walk through the town and make sure that everything was safely locked up at night. As few families could afford clocks, the watchmen would also call out the time.

In many towns little groups of watchmen formed musical bands. At Christmas time the waits would go through the town playing carols and other Christmas music. Sometimes they would be invited into a wealthy home to be given good Christmas cheer—cakes, ale, mince pies and, if they were lucky, money.

Waits bands were once quite common in England but in the nineteenth century the police force became much stronger and many towns no longer needed their waits as watchmen. Gradually the bands died out, and by mid-century they had all but disappeared. However, the old custom of group carol singing was not entirely lost. Many churches sent carol singers around the houses to collect for charity, a tradition that is very much alive today.

A 'living' *crèche* near the French town of Chablis.

Waits bands (groups of town watchmen) singing carols were a common sight in the eighteenth and early nineteenth century.

Handel's *Messiah*

Of all Christmas music, George Frideric Handel's oratorio, the *Messiah*, is probably the most popular. It was a smash hit from its very first performance in 1741, and for 250 years since it has been a great Christmas tradition.

Handel wrote the *Messiah* at lightning speed. He began it on Saturday 22 August 1741 at his London home, 25 Brook Street, and finished it in only twenty-four days. There were 256 pages of manuscript covered in alterations, blots and scratchings out.

The words of the *Messiah* were written by Charles Jennings, who was described by the great writer Samuel Johnson as 'a vain fool crazed by his wealth who, were he in Heaven, would criticize the Lord Almighty'. Handel was the very opposite, modest and very kind, especially to children. In fact, at the request of the Duke of Devonshire, who was Lord Lieutenant of Ireland, Handel wrote the *Messiah* for the benefit of charities in Ireland.

The first performance

Handel held the first rehearsal of the *Messiah* in the Golden Falcon at Chester, an inn that was on his route to Ireland where he was to give the work its first full performance.

On 23 December 1741, Handel conducted his new work with thirty-six musicians and about twenty-four singers at Mr Neal's Musick Hall in Dublin. It was an immediate success, as is confirmed by one local newspaper of the time:

'The hall was crowded ... The performance was superior to anything of the kind in the kingdom before ... Words are wanting to express the exquisite Delight it afforded the admiring Crowd.'

George Frideric Handel wrote the *Messiah* in only twenty-four days.

Carol singing to raise a little money for ➤ Christmas treats.

Ⅴ The original manuscript of the *Messiah*. Handel gave it to his favourite charity, the Foundling Hospital in London.

Handel was a governor of the Foundling Hospital in London which helped poor and orphaned children, and he gave performances of the *Messiah* there every year until 1754. He then presented the original score to the hospital.

The *Messiah* grows and grows

In 1784 there was a special performance of the *Messiah* in Westminster Abbey, but by now with no less than 253 players and 257 singers. The crowd was so huge that those who could not get in threatened to break down the doors of the Abbey.

In 1857 Queen Victoria, Prince Albert and about 20,000 people attended a performance at the Crystal Palace, London. By this time the orchestra had grown to 500 and the number of singers to 2000.

A performance at Chicago in 1900 had 1000 musicians and 1000 singers, and it became a yearly event in the city. The taste for ever bigger numbers of performers reached its peak in 1910 when it was staged with no fewer than 5000 singers at the Crystal Palace.

The American conductor David Randolph claims the world record for performing the *Messiah*. He has conducted the work more than 150 times.

The beginnings of pantomime

Pantomime is a very British tradition. Nothing quite like it is found elsewhere in Europe or in America, but its roots go beyond the shores of the British Isles.

The word 'pantomime' is made up of two Greek words. The root *panto-* means 'all kinds' and *mimos* is a type of silent acting which we still know today as 'mime'. This, then, was an entertainment without words, in which actors (including men dressed as women and women dressed as men) took part in different kinds of comic scenes that included juggling and clowning.

These silent comedies were enjoyed particularly during the Roman Saturnalia festivities. The Roman tradition of mime would certainly have been brought to Britain during the Roman occupation.

Panto from Italy

In Italy, from the sixteenth to the eighteenth century, there was a type of theatre called *commedia dell'arte* which, as its name suggests, was a form of comedy. One of the main characters was Arlecchino, who in Britain became Harlequin, a favourite pantomime hero in the Victorian age. Other *commedia* characters were a young woman named Columbina, a crusty old villain called Pantalone, and a fool or clown named Zani. Gradually all these characters found their way, in one guise or another, into pantomime.

The great age of pantomime

Something resembling pantomime, featuring knockabout comic characters, could already be seen in eighteenth-century England, but it was during the Victorian age that pantomime as we know it became the most popular of all Christmas entertainments for children.

Some of these pantomime shows still centred around Harlequin, a character who has now completely disappeared. For example, there was 'Harlequin and Jack the Giant Killer' and the tongue-twisting 'Harlequin and Pooonoowingkeewongflibeedeebuskeebang, King of the Cannibal Islands'. But gradually something more like a modern 'variety show' took over. The story did not matter much as long as there were plenty of jugglers, acrobats, comedians, and songs.

Pantomime was the favourite Christmas entertainment of Victorian Britain.

The Italian *commedia dell' arte* was a type of comic theatre, elements of which
found their way into British pantomime.

Pantomime stories

Many of the pantomimes staged today are based on very old stories. 'Babes in the Wood', for example, first appeared in England about 500 years ago. It was derived from a popular poem called 'The Children in the Wood, or the Norfolk Gentleman's Last Will and Testament'.

'Puss in Boots' and 'The Sleeping Beauty' are over 450 years old. They come from the fairy stories of Charles Perrault, a sixteenth-century French writer.

In 1717 the *Arabian Nights* stories were translated into English. Some of these tales were turned into pantomimes: they include 'Ali Baba and the Forty Thieves', 'Aladdin and His Magic Lantern', and 'Sinbad the Sailor'.

'Dick Whittington', 'Robinson Crusoe', and 'Robin Hood' were all Victorian creations, based on familiar characters of fiction, and are as popular today as they were then.

An Edwardian memory

F. Gordon Roe described his first visit to a pantomime in 1902:

> 'It was "Sinbad the Sailor" at the Grand
> Theatre, Fulham . . . I was thrilled to the
> core. Especially when Agrippa, the Old
> Man of the Sea, greenly glowing in fear-
> some make-up . . . pulled down the ship
> to her doom. He looked to me so incredi-
> bly evil that I awoke crying out in the
> night.'

The Grand Theatre, Fulham, London, 1898.

Party games

> 'When they were all tired of blind man's buff,
> there was a great game of snapdragon, and
> when fingers were burned with that, and all the
> raisins were gone, they sat down by a huge fire
> of blazing logs.'
>
> Charles Dickens, *The Pickwick Papers*

'Snapdragon' was one of the most popular party
games in Victorian times. Judging from descriptions,
it was quite dangerous and definitely not something
that parents would approve of today.

A bowl was filled with brandy and currants, and
the brandy was then set alight. The players had to try
to snatch currants from the burning brandy and eat
them. The currants were alight. The trick was to close
your mouth quickly once you had popped them in.

One version of Blind Man's Buff was called Queen
of Sheba. A girl sat in a chair in the middle of the
room. A young man was blindfolded and twirled
around until he had no idea which way he was facing.
He then had to find the girl and give her a kiss. While
he was searching, the young girl's place was taken by
an old woman, much to the young man's embarrass-
ment when he finally planted his kiss and pulled off
the blindfold.

Dames and principal boys

Widow Twankey is still the most popular of all the
pantomime 'dames'. And she is, of course, always
played by a man, usually a well-known comedian of
stage or television. The character was originally
Aladdin's mother and called the Widow Ching
Mustapha, but by 1870 she adopted the name of
Twankey, taken from a type of tea, called 'twankei',
which was first brought to England from China in the
nineteenth century.

The 'principal boy' in the pantomime, on the other
hand, is always played by a girl. He is usually supposed
to be a handsome prince, and he was first introduced
into pantomime in the 1880s by Augustus Harris, the
manager of London's Drury Lane Theatre.

Les Dawson, a well-known English comedian, appears in
Dick Whittington as 'Ada the Cook', one of the famous
pantomime 'dames'.

'Cinderella' was one of the most popular Victorian pantomimes.

Children playing the game snapdragon.

A Victorian view of Christmas merry-making, eighteenth-century style.

Boxing Day

Boxing Day is very much a British tradition, going back many centuries but only made an official holiday in 1871. Known also as St Stephen's Day, it was customarily a time for giving to the poor.

The name comes partly from the boxes kept in churches to collect money for the needy. On the day after Christmas Day these boxes were opened and the money shared among the poor people of the parish. The churches also gave food and clothing to those in need.

There used to be a tradition of 'Stephening' at the church of Drayton Beauchamp in Buckinghamshire. The villagers went to the vicar's house and expected to be given as much bread, cheese, and ale as they could eat—at his expense! One year the vicar refused to give the villagers their traditional 'Christmas box'. In disgust they broke into his house and ate and drank all they could find. By 1834 the local tradition of 'Stephening' had ended because the parish had grown too large.

Workmen and young apprentices also had Christmas 'boxes' made of pottery, which they would take to their masters' customers and ask for money. On Boxing Day the pottery boxes were smashed and the money was then spent by the workmen on food and drink.

In many countries it is still traditional to offer a gift of money at Christmas to people who provide services during the year, such as the boy or girl who delivers the newspapers.

The Christmas cracker was a Victorian invention.

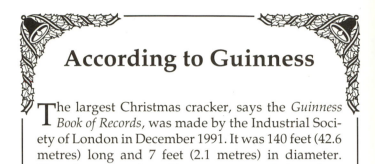

According to Guinness

The largest Christmas cracker, says the *Guinness Book of Records*, was made by the Industrial Society of London in December 1991. It was 140 feet (42.6 metres) long and 7 feet (2.1 metres) in diameter. There is no mention of how many people it took to pull it, but pull it they did!

Boxing Day has always been a day for fun. In olden times there would be horse races, boxing matches or even cock-fights, and this link with sport still survives today in Britain. For example, there is a full programme of soccer, often featuring matches between local rivals which give the Boxing Day games a particular edge.

Christmas crackers

The first illustration of a Christmas cracker appeared in *The Illustrated London News* in 1847, but there is some argument as to who should be credited with this very British invention. Until recently, two Christmas cracker manufacturers, Tom Smith & Co. and James Hovell & Co., claimed that their founders had made the great discovery. In 1985 the companies merged, so the argument is no longer as heated as it once was.

Tom Smith (or James Hovell, if you prefer) was a London sweet maker and seller. In the 1840s he went to Paris where he saw sweets called 'bon-bons' wrapped in twists of brightly coloured paper. He brought back the idea and added a twist of his own. Inside each wrapping he put a little slip of paper with a message on it. They were called 'kiss mottoes'. Later, other attractions were added in the form of little paper hats, tokens and small toys. And there was a further surprise.

The crack in the cracker

Tom Smith, or James Hovell, was apparently sitting in front of his Christmas fire one year. The yule logs were crackling, and they gave him the idea of putting a 'cracker' strip inside his bon-bons, so that they made a sharp snapping sound when pulled from either end. The term 'cracker' was used to describe this improved bon-bon. The crackers were also made to look like tiny yule logs, as they still do today.

'The best Christmas dinner of my life'

By Christmas Day 1870, the French capital of Paris had been besieged by the Prussian army for ninety-eight days. Almost all the food had gone. Even the animals in the zoo had been eaten. An American officer who was in the city as an observer described his Christmas dinner:

'Never has a sadder Christmas dawned on any city. Cold and hunger sit enthroned in every house. The sufferings of the past week exceed anything we have seen so far. However, a few of us determined to enjoy Christmas as best we could. There is hardly any meat except horsemeat, and precious little of that. A little poultry remains at fabulous prices. A goose was $25 and a chicken $7 [about fifteen times their normal price at the time].

'Having no fuel we set off for one of the few restaurants that were still able to offer a meal. The owner was surprisingly jolly and said indeed he could set before us a delicious Christmas dinner. It would not be turkey, or goose or even a fat chicken, but something he called *petit lièvre de Paris. Lièvre* is hare, and although not traditional at Christmas, made our mouths water in anticipation.

'In a trice there came to table a silver covered dish. The aroma which issued from it was delicious and tantalizing. The cover removed, we saw a fine fricassee of *lièvre* and herbs in a rich sauce. I can only tell you that it tasted as good as it smelled and looked. In a short time the only remaining evidence of our meal was a few whitened bones decorating our plates. We could have eaten it three times over, and indeed offered to! But the owner, shrugging his shoulders sadly, declared that his supply of hare was, alas, limited and that there were other customers who would be sorely disappointed if he sold all his plump little beasts to us.

'A week later our trusty servant, Henri, was walking behind the restaurant in which we had taken our fine Christmas dinner. There he saw three young ruffians skinning rats. He asked them what they were about. "Sir," they replied, "we catches 'em good and fat down the sewers then sells 'em to the likes of this restaurant where ignorant bodies pay good money to eat what they think is hare!" They even went on to recite their little rhyme:

'"Rats are not a dainty dish to set before a king,
But for a really hungry man they're just the very thing.
Wrap each rat in tasty fat, roast slow before the fire,
Take him down and serve him brown; you've all you can desire."

'It is now many years since those days of terrible hardship. Yet there is many a Christmas when, sitting down to a golden roast turkey with all the trimmings, I cannot help but think with longing of my little "hares" of Paris!'

Week ending December 22 1951   Wednesday Fourpence

John Bull

CHRISTMAS TREE PAINTING
IN BRILLIANT COLOUR
Presented to every reader—page 14

HOLIDAY STORIES AND JOKES

5

CHRISTMAS THIS CENTURY

The Christmas saint

Hundreds of years ago children in Europe looked forward to receiving their Christmas gifts from St Nicholas. He was based on the real character of St Nicholas of Myra (see page 45), and was usually shown as a rather thin, pale figure dressed in his bishop's robes of a red cassock and white surplice. He also wore a mitre, the traditional hat of a bishop, and he carried a crozier, a bishop's ceremonial staff.

Unlike the modern image of Father Christmas or Santa Claus, St Nicholas did not travel by sleigh drawn by a team of reindeer but by a much slower form of transport, a donkey. Nor did he deliver his gifts on Christmas Eve, but on his feast day, 6 December. Sometimes he was shown riding a white horse, like the god Odin whom St Nicholas had replaced when Christianity drove paganism out of northern Europe.

Santa Claus and Father Christmas

The old St Nicholas was much loved in Europe and when the Dutch went to America in the seventeenth century they naturally took him along. In fact, the first Dutch ship to land at Nieuw (New) Amsterdam, later to become New York, had a carving of St Nicholas, patron saint of children and sailors, on its prow. And the first church built by the Dutch in Nieuw Amsterdam was named for St Nicholas.

The original Dutch settlers in America spelled St Nicholas 'Sint Nikolaas', which gradually changed into 'Sinterklaas'. As more and more English colo-

Groeten van St. Nicolaas!

St Nicholas, as imagined about 1900.

◁ The cover of *John Bull*, December 1951.

nists took over from the Dutch, 'Sinterklaas' turned into 'Santa Claus'.

St Nicholas has always been a much more popular figure in Europe than in Britain, where people preferred Father Christmas, a jolly character first seen in the mumming plays of the Middle Ages. And when Santa Claus became popular in the nineteenth century, he and Father Christmas gradually merged.

Kriss Kringle

The German settlers who reached America in the early nineteenth century took with them their own Christmas traditions, one of which was that of the 'Christkind', an angelic child sent by Jesus to bring gifts to good children. Naughty children were visited by two scary little elves, Knecht Rupprecht and

Thomas Nast's first published Santa Claus illustration, 1863.

The cover of Dr Clement Moore's poem. The poem's proper title is 'A Visit from St Nicholas'.

The Christmas elves, Knecht Rupprecht and Pelznickol, as shown on a German Christmas card of about 1910.

A Visit from St Nicholas

'T was the night before Christmas, when all through the house
Not a creature was stirring, not even a mouse.
The stockings were hung by the chimney with care,
In hopes that St Nicholas soon would be there.
The children were nestled all snug in their beds,
While visions of sugar-plums danced in their heads;
And mamma in kerchief, and I in my cap,
Had just settled our brains for a long winter's nap—
When out on the lawn there arose such a clatter
I sprang from my bed to see what was the matter.
Away to the window I flew like a flash,
Tore open the shutter, and threw up the sash.
The moon on the breast of the new-fallen snow
Gave a lustre of midday to objects below;
When what to my wondering eye should appear
But a miniature sleigh and eight tiny reindeer,
With a little old driver, so lively and quick,
I knew in a moment it must be St Nick!
More rapid than eagles his coursers they came,
And he whistled and shouted and called them by name.
'Now, Dasher! now, Dancer! now, Prancer and Vixen!
On, Comet! on, Cupid! on Donner and Blitzen!—
To the top of the porch, to the top of the wall,
Now, dash away, dash away, dash away all!'
As dry leaves that before the wild hurricane fly,
When they meet with an obstacle mount to the sky,
So, to the housetop the coursers they flew,
With a sleigh full of toys—and St Nicholas too.
And then, in a twinkling, I heard on the roof
The prancing and pawing of each little hoof.
As I drew in my head and was turning around,

Down the chimney St Nicholas came with a bound:
He was dressed all in fur from his head to his foot,
And his clothes were all tarnished with ashes and soot:
A bundle of toys he had flung on his back,
And he looked like a peddler just opening his pack.
His eyes, how they twinkled! his dimples, how merry!
His cheeks were like roses, his nose like a cherry;
His droll little mouth was drawn up like a bow,
And the beard on his chin was as white as the snow.
The stump of a pipe he held tight in his teeth,
And the smoke, it encircled his head like a wreath.
He had a broad face and a round little belly
That shook when he laughed like a bowl full of jelly.
He was chubby and plump—a right jolly old elf:
And I laughed when I saw him, in spite of myself;
A wink of his eye, and a twist of his head,
Soon gave me to know I had nothing to dread.
He spoke not a word, but went straight to his work,
And filled all the stockings: then turned with a jerk,
And laying his finger aside of his nose,
And giving a nod, up the chimney he rose.
He sprang to his sleigh, to his team gave a whistle,
And away they all flew like the down of a thistle.
But I heard him exclaim, ere they drove out of sight,
'Happy Christmas to all, and to all a good night!'

95

Pelznickol. As the years went by, Christkind, Knecht Rupprecht, and Pelznickol turned into the merry elfin gift-bringer, Kriss Kringle.

The poem that launched Santa

In America, the familiar image of Santa Claus, in word and picture, was fostered by three men in particular: Dr Clement Moore, Thomas Nast and Haddon Sundblom.

On 23 December 1822, Dr Clement Moore, a university professor, decided to write a Christmas poem for his children. He called it 'A Visit from St Nicholas', but it became better known by its opening words: ''Twas the night before Christmas'. The St Nicholas of the poem is a jolly red-cheeked elf, quite unlike the rather solemn bishop-saint of earlier times.

Dr Moore never meant the poem for publication, for as a teacher, he feared he would be ridiculed for writing children's verse. However, a friend sent a copy to a newspaper. Very soon the poem had become famous across the United States. But it was not until 1838 that Dr Moore owned up to having written it.

The association of Santa Claus and chimneys goes back to the original legend of St Nicholas of Myra, see page 45.

Thomas Nast's Santas became jollier and fatter as the years passed. This one is from 1881.

The cartoonist Thomas Nast began to illustrate Clement Moore's St Nicholas for *Harper's Weekly* magazine in 1863.

At first Nast drew him as a mischievous little elf, as described in the poem. But as the years passed, the drawings changed. St Nicholas became taller and fatter, his beard grew bushier, but he was still dressed in a plain suit of fur, exactly as the poem said.

The Coca-Cola saint

Santa Claus, as we know him today, with a great white beard, red tunic, hat and trousers trimmed with white fur, high black boots, and a beaming red-cheeked face, was created by an American commercial artist, Haddon Sundblom. In 1931 Sundblom was commissioned by the Coca-Cola Company to illustrate their Christmas advertising. So successful

The Coca-Cola Santa, first created by artist Haddon Sundblom in 1931.

'Temptation in the toy department',
from *Colliers* magazine,
December 1956.

was the Coca-Cola Santa Claus that he became a Christmas tradition, not only in America, but around the world.

Down the chimney

It seems strange that poor old Santa has to go to all the trouble of climbing down the chimney and does not just come through the front door like anyone else. Two legends explain the custom. The first has to do with St Nicholas of Myra who, as we have seen, dropped his bags of gold down the chimney and into the stockings of the poor family he was helping. The other story, much older, concerns Hertha, the German pagan goddess of the home. During the winter solstice each house would be decorated with fir boughs and other evergreens to welcome her. A plat-

form of stones, like an altar, was built in the hearth (our word comes from her name) and evergreens burned on it. Hertha was believed to come down through the smoke of the blazing branches, rewarding the good and punishing the bad.

Rules for Santa Claus

For many children, especially in towns and cities, an extra seasonal treat is a visit to Father Christmas or Santa Claus in his Toyland Grotto, tucked away inside a big department store.

Anyone who thinks that playing Santa is a 'piece of cake' should take to heart a list of rules drawn up by Donovan and Fields, a Chicago department store, in 1932:

Rules for Santa Claus

To: Mrs Niska Woodenhof, Personnel Manager.
From: Hampson S. Sisler, General Manager.
Re: Store Santa Claus.

It has been brought to my attention that certain acts of negligence and misconduct by members of the corps of Santa Clauses has greatly embarrassed our customers and jeopardized our good reputation.

Instance. Norbert Cleeverhook was found to be inebriated [drunk] while on duty during the afternoon shift last Wednesday. He attacked one child and swore at the parent who intervened. Cleeverhook has, as you know, been dismissed.

Instance. Donald J. McPhearson has been severely reprimanded for taking a gratuity [tip] of $2 from a parent.

Instance. Harold Jones, relief Santa, was heard complaining to several children and parents that he had not had a break for over two hours and intended to report us to the Mayor's Commission on Fair Working Practices.

It is of the greatest importance that we endeavour to employ only men of the highest dependability to act as our 'Christmas ambassadors'. Will you please ensure that the following points are impressed upon all staff engaged in this most delicate of Christmas operations. These ten rules are to be considered the indispensable 'Steps to Good Santahood':

1. Bodily hygiene is to be scrupulous. Special attention should be paid to the cleanliness of undergarments and socks.

2. Ditto oral hygiene. Please ask Santas to refrain from eating strong-smelling foods such as garlic. Chewing-tobacco is to be discouraged.

3. Fingernails are to be kept short and clean. Outgrowths of nasal hair will not be tolerated.

4. Santas must ensure that tunics, boots, beards and wigs are kept clean. An overnight laundry service will be provided.

5. Please ensure that correctly fitting uniforms are issued and that all tears, lost buttons etc. are promptly repaired.

6. Under *no* circumstances may intoxicating beverages be consumed on the premises or prior to Santas taking up their duties. The penalty shall be instant dismissal.

7. Santas may not congregate in uniform by the Staff entrance when off-duty or smoke cigarettes or cigars when off-duty and in view of the passing public. They must use the Staff rest area for such purposes.

8. No gratuities may be accepted from parents.

9. Santas shall adopt an appropriate tone of voice and demeanour when addressing children. They shall not use low, slang expressions. Nor shall they, on pain of instant dismissal, abuse either verbally or physically any child or guardian.

10. Should an emergency occur, such as a child losing control or being sick over a Santa, then a relief will assume his duties *without delay*. Will you please ensure that adequate Santa relief is available at all times.

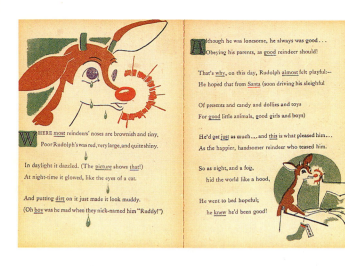

The original poem and illustrations for 'Rudolph the
Red-Nosed Reindeer', 1939.

Quick reindeer facts

- Reindeer are the only species of deer in which both
  sexes have antlers.
- On average, they weigh 600 pounds (300 kilograms) and are about 5 feet (1.8 metres) at the
  shoulder.
- In Lapland they are used as pack animals as well
  as for milk, skins and meat.
- They have very broad hooves which make travelling over snow easier.
- They do not have red noses.

'Once a Year' (1966) by Gerald Gooch: from ordinary mortal to
Santa Claus in ten steps.

'More rapid than eagles his coursers they came.
And he whistled and shouted and called them by name.
"Now, Dasher! now, Dancer! now, Prancer and Vixen!
On, Comet! on, Cupid! on, Donner and Blitzen!"'

Reginald the red-nosed reindeer

In 1939 Robert May, who worked in the advertising section of the Montgomery Ward department store in Chicago, came up with an idea for a new kind of Christmas gift for children. He wrote a poem about one of Santa's deer with an illuminated red nose who helped his master find his way from chimney to chimney. The author suggested the name Rollo for his leading deer, but it was rejected. He next thought of Reginald, and that, too, was turned down. Finally he came up with—Rudolph!

In that first Christmas, every child who visited the store's resident Santa received a booklet of 'Rudolph the Red-Nosed Reindeer'. More than 2.4 million copies were given away free.

Rudolph tops the hit parade

In 1949 Johnny Marks, a friend of Robert May, decided to set the poem to music. He approached various singers to record it, without success. Finally, Gene Autry, the popular Western film star and radio singer, agreed. The record zoomed to the top of the hit parade. Next to Bing Crosby's 'White Christmas', Autry's version of 'Rudolph the Red-Nosed Reindeer' is the second biggest-selling record of *all time*! Since then there have been over 300 versions of the song, and more than 80 million records sold.

Christmas on the streets

Although this is the story of one homeless person's Christmas on the streets of New York, it could just as easily be London, Paris, Los Angeles or any one of thousands of our towns and cities.

Billy 'Happy' Boyd has lived on the streets of New York for more than eight years. He is fifty-one years old. His 'home' is a large sheet of cardboard placed over a warm-air outlet of the subway at 12th Street and Seventh Avenue. He will not go to a city-run shelter for the homeless because they are dangerous places where hundreds of men like him sleep in huge dormitories. There are often fights, and the last time 'Happy' went to one he had his nose broken and his only pair of shoes stolen. This is what he says about Christmas:

'A Christmas Puzzle', 1895. The shivering boy has just told a puzzled Father Christmas that he has no stocking to hang up to receive a gift. In fact he has no stockings to wear at all.

'I have all mixed feelings about Christmas. It makes me think of when I was a boy, living in Brooklyn. My folks didn't have much money and we were a big family—nine kids! But we always had a good time at Christmas. In those days everything was much friendlier than now. All the families in my neighborhood, and it was a tough neighborhood, knew each other. We enjoyed ourselves together and if one family had no money at Christmas to buy food, they'd always get given something or get invited to someone's place for Christmas dinner. Now it makes me sad to think about it. I sometimes think there's no one in this whole wide world who cares if I live or die. That's a heavy thought to carry around.

'For about ten days before Christmas people open their pockets a bit more. Once a lady came up and gave me $20 [about £13] when I was singing a carol, and she said, "Have a very happy Christmas." It's not just the money. You want to be spoken to like a regular human being. The little kids are the best. They don't turn their noses up and look the other way. And when I say, "Happy Christmas" they say, "Happy Christmas" right back, even though their parents don't like it much. Sometimes the kids will say to their mom or dad, "Is that man cold? Is he hungry?" One kid came right up to me and said, "Mister, do you want to come to my house?" His mom looked like a brick had fallen on her head! In their way I think the kids are worried for me, even if it is only for a little while.

'On Christmas day I always do something special. The best place is the Salvation Army where they give you a big Christmas dinner—turkey and all the trimmings—and they treat you like a real proper human being. It's not like the other shelters where you line up for your food. The Army has tables with clean table-cloths. And people serve you! Somebody serves *me*!

'I think I'm tough. You have to be to make it out here. But every year round that table I cry when we sing carols. And I'm not the only one! It's like everything comes together. All the memories. On the street you're always being hassled, or worse, and when people are kind sometimes you just kind of snap. But I always say, "Hey, c'mon, Happy, cheer up. It's only 364 days to Christmas!"'

The royal Christmas

The British Royal Family, like most families, spend their Christmases with relatives and close friends. But there are one or two special traditions and customs that set the royal Christmas apart.

On one of the evenings leading up to Christmas, Harrods, the famous London department store, closes early so that members of the Royal Family may shop uninterrupted by the normal throng of Christmas shoppers. Gifts are bought both for relatives and for everyone belonging to the royal household.

The royal Christmas is spent either at Windsor Castle or at Sandringham. One unusual custom dates back to Queen Alexandra, wife of King Edward VII, who began the tradition of opening the royal gifts on Christmas Eve. The Queen enters with a trolley piled with presents. A huge white-clothed table is divided and subdivided by a scarlet ribbon. Each member of the Royal Family is allocated a space on the table. Not all the gifts will be expensive for there are usually a few carefully chosen joke ones.

On Christmas Day, after the morning service, lunch is taken promptly at 1.15 pm. The first course is lobster soup followed by roast turkey with vegetables. A Christmas pudding, flaming with hot brandy, ends the meal at 3 pm, in time for the Royal Family to sit down to watch the Queen's speech which has been pre-recorded.

A cartoonist's view of Christmas with the Royal Family.

Boxing Day is set aside for shooting, unless it happens to fall on a Sunday, and there are further celebrations during the following week.

A Scandinavian Christmas

It was here in the old land of the Norsemen that many of our Christmas traditions began. And probably nowhere else is Christmas celebrated today as warmly as in Scandinavia. Preparations start weeks beforehand, usually with the cooking of Christmas biscuits, known as *pebbernodder* in Denmark and *pepparkakor* in Sweden. Other specialities, found throughout Scandinavia, are ribbons of dough, *klener* or *klenatter*, deep fried in fat. And because so many Scandinavians—Swedes, Norwegians and Danes—went to America in the nineteenth century, taking their customs with them, much of the modern American Christmas has a Scandinavian flavour.

Typical Christmas treats, from a Danish magazine of 1921.

Old customs

Scandinavian Christmas celebrations, both at home and across the Atlantic, were big and happy. Reading about them, we can almost see the Vikings gulping down hornfuls of ale and tucking into a roast ox. This is how an American Norwegian woman remembered her Christmases back in the 'old country' in the middle of the nineteenth century:

'People started their preparations for Christmas in October. They slaughtered as many as twenty or thirty sheep on the big farms . . . At Martinmas [11 November] it was the turn of the geese, then the pigs, and an ox or large cow. They made masses of brawn, sausages, and black pudding. The walls and ceilings of the pantry were crammed to overflowing with jars, pans and barrels filled with all sorts of provisions such as honey, butter, lard, and goose fat.

'There were always many many people to the Christmas feast, so we distilled several hundred gallons of aquavit [a very strong drink]. The candles were dipped and then all the women set about doing a really big wash.

'The big occasion was Christmas Eve. Friends and neighbours came from all around—maybe 100 of us all together. In those days we had big families! In the middle of the table was a wooden platter piled high with ham, pigs' trotters, sausage, mutton and pork—and this was just to start the meal.

'The main course began with bread and butter spread with goose fat. Then there would be other sausages and meats—all washed down with aquavit and beer. Next came a dish of browned cabbage. Then the *lutfisk* [cod preserved in a solution of lime] which was always served with plenty of mustard and boiled potatoes. By now everybody was groaning a little bit. But there was always room for the buckwheat porridge with cream as well as the pastries and coffee to round off the whole feast.'

The modern way

Although the main Christmas celebration is on Christmas Eve, it is nowhere near as massive a meal as the one just described. There will almost certainly be a *smörgasbord*, a collection of fish and meat dishes, which means that everyone takes a little piece of this and a little bit of that: just like a medieval banquet!

Another speciality is a ham with apple-sauce; and a great Scandinavian tradition, called *doppa i grytan*, is to dip pieces of bread into the water in which the ham has been boiled. This reminds people that winters in the past were hard and that no food, not even the water in which it had been cooked, was to be wasted.

A Swedish family's Christmas meal is served buffet-style in this nineteenth-century illustration.

Joulupukki, Julemand and Jul-Nisse

In Finland the *joulupukki* (Christmas elves) arrive by sleigh and leave the children's gifts under the tree. In Denmark the Christmas presents are brought by *Julemand* (literally 'Yule Man' or Father Christmas). Here, too, you are expected to leave a little snack for the *Jul-Nisse*, the friendly little elf who lives in the attic and can only be seen by the family cat. The *Jul-Nisse*'s Christmas treat is usually a bowl of porridge, which is traditional throughout Scandinavia at this season.

The Swedish custom of the Feast of St Lucia, seen here being celebrated in the middle of the nineteenth century.

The Feast of St Lucia

A Swedish legend tells of St Lucia who, during a terrible famine, miraculously kept the people alive by handing out food. Her memory is honoured on 13 December, the real beginning of the Christmas season in Sweden. On this day most of the shops, schools, and offices choose a girl to be their own 'St Lucia Bride'.

At home the eldest daughter takes the part of the 'Bride'. She dresses in a flowing white dress with a red sash. On her head she wears a crown of evergreens in which there are seven candles. On the morning of St Lucia's Day it is traditional for the 'Lucia Bride' to bring coffee and little cakes to her parents in bed.

A Dutch Christmas

In Holland, St Nicholas' Day, 6 December, is when children receive their gifts, provided, of course, they have been good. Throughout the year Sinterklaas, St Nicholas, has been keeping a note of good and bad behaviour in his great red book. On Sinterklaas Eve he checks through his records while his servant, Piet, gets the gifts ready. There is no freezing sleigh ride for the Dutch Sinterklaas. Legend says that he comes from Spain by steamboat!

The dining table is set on the evening of 5 December and each place is marked with a large chocolate initial. Then the children have to find their presents— no simple matter because they have to solve clues.

The gifts do not have to be prettily wrapped but they should be difficult to open or hard to discover. The present might be buried in a glove full of sand or it might turn up only after following a trail of clues through the house. When the children find their gifts they shout out, 'Thank you, Sinterklaas!'

Lights and bells

In Holland there are candles and lights in every home, and the Christmas tree sparkles with glass bells, little wreaths (*kransies*) and, to top it all off, a beautiful glass ornament called a *piek*. On Christmas Eve families and friends get together, put their presents under the tree and all sit down to enjoy Christmas dinner.

On Christmas morning there is usually a special breakfast which will include a fruit loaf, the *kerstbrood*. With any luck there will be food left over from the previous evening and perhaps a slice or two from the *kersttulband*, the traditional Christmas cake with a hole in the middle.

On 26 December the Christmas tree must be taken down and left outside the door. Children will take it away and add it to all the others on the Christmas bonfires.

Decorating the *Christbaum* (Christmas tree) in Germany during the nineteenth century.

A German Christmas

The Christmas season starts with the first Sunday in Advent, four weeks before Christmas Day. An Advent wreath is made of fir-tree branches and decorated with scarlet ribbon and four candles. On this and each of the three successive Sundays the family gather to light a candle.

Here, too, the traditional day for giving presents is 6 December. 'Nikolas', drawn in a sleigh by a donkey, puts his gifts in shoes and boots that have been brightly polished and placed on a windowsill.

Christmas Eve

In many towns there is a special Christmas market, *Weinachtsmarkte*, selling fruit, sweets and small gifts. Traditionally it is the *Weinachtsmann* (Father Christmas) who brings the presents, but in some areas they are brought by the *Christkind* or Christmas child. On Christmas Eve the whole family gathers round the beautifully decorated tree to open their gifts.

No Christmas would be complete without special cakes and biscuits. The rich *stollen* cake, containing dried fruit and candied peel, is probably the most famous. *Pfeffernusse*, a type of gingerbread, gives the whole family a chance to make a contribution as everyone is expected to stir the dough. *Lebkuchen*, (honey cake) and *sprengerle* (an aniseed-flavoured cake) are also an important part of the traditional German Christmas.

An Italian Christmas

The tradition of having a Christmas crib or *presepio* in every home or church is typically Italian. As we have seen (page 83), the custom was started by St Francis of Assisi in 1223, and each tiny model manger has its three Wise Men, Holy Family, shepherds and a good number of angels. In many churches, however, the Nativity scene will be made of human and animal models, about half life-size.

The legend of La Befana

In Italy it is the old fairy, La Befana, who brings the children their Christmas gifts. The story goes that she was a lonely old widow at the time of Christ's birth.

Pretzels

On a freezing day in, for example, New York or Chicago the smell of hot pretzels, a kind of savoury bread-biscuit, is enough to make the mouth water. They are sold from little street-corner carts and are kept hot over glowing charcoal. Not many Americans would associate them particularly with Christmas, but their distinctive shape goes far back to an ancient German custom.

The pagan sign for the winter solstice was a circle with a dot in the centre. The bread baked during the solstice festivities was called *bretzel*. Originally the *bretzel* was a circle of dough with a cross of dough in the middle. This shape was meant to show the year divided into the four seasons. Today's pretzels have exactly the same shape, but not many people realize they are eating a pagan symbol of the winter solstice!

Her only child had died of the plague and in order to keep her mind off her grief she busied herself with household tasks.

In New York hot pretzels are sold from street-corner carts. Pretzels are a pagan symbol of the winter solstice.

refused the chance to travel to Bethlehem because she was too busy around the house. Both Befana and Baboushka get their names from 'Epiphany', 6 January, the day the Wise Men gave their gifts to Jesus. And in Italy Christmas Day takes second place to the Feast of the Epiphany, although it is still a time to enjoy a good meal, perhaps with traditional Christmas cakes such as *panettone*, *pandoro* and *torrone*.

A Sicilian Christmas

An old tradition in Sicily at Christmas was for shepherds to come down from the mountains into the towns and villages. Playing bagpipes, drums and violins, they would wind their way among the houses.

An old Sicilian custom: shepherds come down from the hills into the towns to play and sing Christmas songs.

La Befana is to the Italian Christmas what Santa Claus is elsewhere.

One day, on their way to Bethlehem, the three Wise Men stopped at her house. Would she like to join them on their journey, they asked? No, she replied, she was much too occupied with her housework.

The next day Befana realized what an opportunity she had missed and set off to try to catch up with the Wise Men. She became hopelessly lost and was doomed for eternity to wander the Earth searching for the Christ child. To make up for her stupidity she fills the stockings of good children with Christmas gifts, flying from house to house on her broomstick. But there is still something of the witch about her, for bad children get their stockings filled with coal! Today, though, sweets which only look like coal are substituted for the real thing.

It is interesting that the legend of Befana also exists in Russia, where she is called Baboushka. She also

A pyramid-shaped altar would be built in each house and church, and on it was placed a baby Jesus made of wax. Each evening for the nine days leading up to Christmas, the altar would be lit as the family gathered round it to say Christmas prayers together.

The tradition still lasts in some country regions. Everywhere, however, as in Italy, midnight mass on Christmas Eve is followed by a procession through the town.

A French Christmas

Preparations for setting up the *crèche* or Christmas crib usually begin two weeks beforehand. Each day more and more figures are added until only one, the infant Jesus, remains. Traditionally he is only placed in the *crèche* on Christmas Eve, which is a more important occasion than Christmas Day.

Children play at giving and receiving *étrennes*, the traditional 'Christmas box' in France.

Along with the *crèche*, most French families decorate a Christmas tree, a custom that only started around 1840. The Duchess of Orléans at that time was Princess Helen of Mecklenburg who, like Prince Albert in England, introduced the tradition from her German homeland. Before that, Christmas trees were generally seen only in those parts of France, such as Alsace and Lorraine, that bordered Germany.

The midnight feast

After celebrating midnight mass, French families often return home or visit a restaurant for a grand Christmas feast known as the *réveillon*. This splendid meal often includes such delicacies as oysters, lobster, a type of sausage called *boudin blanc*, and roast truffled turkey. There may also be special Christmas cakes such as *pain d'épices*, a spicy kind of gingerbread, and the famous *bûche de Noël*, a cake in the shape of a yule log.

After the *réveillon* French children will put shoes, slippers or, if they are really greedy, big boots in front of the fire. During the night, Père Noël (Father Christmas) comes along and fills them with *étrennes* or gifts.

The word *étrennes* was originally applied to the New Year presents that children gave their parents. It also meant the gift of money or 'Christmas box' that people gave to postal workers, the concierge or caretaker, and so on. But now *étrennes* means either Christmas or New Year presents.

A Japanese Christmas

The Japanese love festivals and although only about one per cent of the population is Christian, Christmas is still widely celebrated as a non-religious holiday. It all began on 24 December 1955 when the Japanese government announced officially that the food shortages caused by the Second World War were over. When they heard the news, a crowd of about one and a half million packed the Ginza, the main street of Tokyo, and every year since then it has become the tradition to celebrate Christmas in the Ginza.

Japanese department stores try hard to promote the idea of Christmas and the custom of giving presents is becoming increasingly popular, as is the figure of Santa Claus.

Christmas in space

On 21 December 1968 the American Apollo 8 spacecraft lifted off from its launch pad at Cape Canaveral, Florida. Its destination was the Moon. Inside the tiny capsule were three astronauts: Frank Borman (commander), James A. Lovell and William Anders. They would be the first humans to orbit the Moon.

The spacecraft reached the cross-over point between the Earth's and the Moon's gravitational fields at 2.29 pm on 23 December. While a quarter of a million miles away, much of the world was preparing for Christmas, the three astronauts circled about 70-150 miles above the surface of the Moon.

During the early part of Christmas Eve, Lovell described the first close-up of the Moon: 'The Moon is essentially grey, no colour. Looks like plaster of Paris. Sort of greyish sand . . .' And shortly afterwards television viewers across the world got their first detailed glimpse of the Moon's surface.

Later on 24 December the spacecraft orbited to the dark side of the Moon, which no human eye had ever seen directly. Anders described it: 'The back side looks like a sand pile my kids have been playing in for a long time. It's all beat up . . . just lots of bumps and holes.'

'Merry Christmas' in sixteen languages

Chinese	*Sheng Dan Kuai Le*
Danish	*Glaedelig Jul*
Dutch	*Froleijk Kerstfeest*
Finnish	*Hanskaa Joulea*
French	*Joyeux Noël*
German	*Fröhliche Weinachten*
Greek	*Kala Christougenna*
Hungarian	*Kellemes Karacsonyi Unnepeket*
Italian	*Buon Natale*
Japanese	*Meri Kurisumasu*
Norwegian	*Gleddelig Jul*
Polish	*Wesolych Swiat*
Portuguese	*Boas Festas*
Russian	*Rozhdestrom Kristovym*
Spanish	*Feliz Navidad*
Swedish	*God Jul*

The Apollo 8 spacecraft lifts off for its Christmas rendezvous with the Moon in 1968.

A message from the Moon

Late on Christmas Eve in America and early on Christmas Day in Europe, the crew of Apollo 8 sent their Christmas message to the millions on Earth watching the flight on television by reading in turn the first five verses of the Book of Genesis: 'In the beginning God created the Heaven and the Earth . . .' It ended with Frank Borman saying, 'And from the crew of Apollo 8 we close with goodnight, good luck, a Merry Christmas, and God bless all of you—all of you on the good Earth.'

On Christmas Day the crew celebrated with a turkey and gravy dinner eaten with a spoon rather than squeezed from a tube, as was most of their food. At Mission Control, back on Earth, they had to be satisfied with sandwiches and coffee!

The time approached for the vital main engine thrust that would send Apollo 8 on its journey back to Earth. If it failed, the crew would be left slowly to suffocate. The engine was ignited and, to everyone's immense relief, exploded into life. James Lovell told Mission Control, 'Please be informed there is a Santa Claus!'

The crew of Apollo 8 took this photograph on Christmas Eve 1968, just before sending the first Christmas message from space to the people of Earth.

Out with the old, in with the new

Some customs have been established for so long that we take them for granted. The New Year, for example, starts on 1 January, as everyone knows. But it was not always so. Many people used to celebrate the New Year at another time, and many still do today.

In fact, the first day of January has no special place in the Sun's or Moon's cycle, nor does it mark the day of the winter solstice. For many centuries the Greeks did indeed begin their New Year on 21 or 22 December, to coincide with the winter solstice. But the ancient Egyptians, Phoenicians and Persians celebrated at the autumn equinox, around 21 September. And the Chinese New Year may fall either in January or February.

Rosh Hashanah

The Jewish New Year, Rosh Hashanah, occurs on a different date each year, either at the end of September or in early October. It is one of the most important religious events of the Jewish calendar and begins the Ten Days of Penitence that end with Yom Kippur or the Day of Atonement, when 'mankind passes in judgement before the heavenly throne'.

At New Year the *shofar*, or sacred ram's horn, is blown like a trumpet in every synagogue, calling the faithful to prayer.

Rosh Hashanah is also a time to celebrate the birth of the world. In the home, to accompany the prayers and the family meal, bread is broken and sliced apples or figs dipped into honey to signify the sweetness that it is hoped will mark the coming year.

Janus and the Roman New Year

People in Europe and America took their New Year from the ancient Roman celebration of Janus, the god of beginnings, from whose name we get 'January'.

Janus also had a special responsibility for doorways. A doorway marks the point at which we move out of one place and, almost at the same time, into another. That is why Janus is always shown with two faces—one facing the past, the other the future.

Even after the coming of Christianity, the old New Year was retained. But in many countries there were

different ideas about the correct date. For example, in twelfth-century England, France and Italy it was 25 March. Only in Spain was 1 January kept as the start of the new year. And it was not until the sixteenth century that this date regained its position in other lands.

New Year in Japan

The Japanese New Year, Shogatsu, is also celebrated on 1 January. It is a time to be with the family, and many Japanese will visit their Buddhist temple or Shinto shrine. There is no general present giving but it is a time for cards, and over 3500 million of them are sent each year. The number of cards received is

A fifteenth-century illustration for January. Here Janus is shown with three faces. Usually he is shown with two: one facing the future, the other the past.

This cover of the *Pears* Christmas annual, 1893, shows a young angel ringing in the New Year.

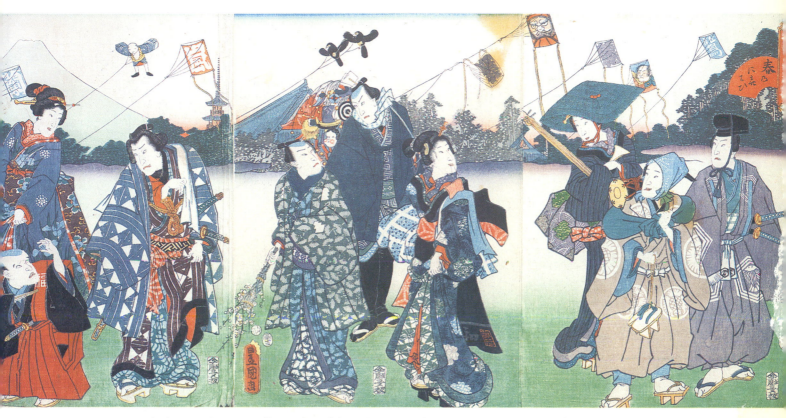

A nineteenth-century illustration of the celebration of the Japanese New Year, Shogatsu.

an indication of a family's importance. It is also the custom at New Year to give young children brand-new bank notes, known as *otoshidama*.

Hogmanay and 'First Footing'

In Scotland, New Year, called Hogmanay, is celebrated with great enthusiasm. One Hogmanay superstition concerns the first person to step into the house in the new year. Who should be the first to set foot over the threshold? All agree that it cannot be anyone with a squint or whose eyebrows meet in the middle, because they will bring bad luck. Preferably it should be a tall, dark-haired man, and he must carry a piece of mistletoe, coal and a coin.

Traditionally, as the clock strikes midnight on New Year's Eve, the family wait in silence for the First Footer's knock. The door is opened and the man walks in without a word. He places the coal on the fire, puts the mistletoe on the mantelpiece and hands the coin to a member of the family. The First Footer then wishes everyone a happy New Year and, with the help of a dram or two, the festivities continue.

As with many traditional customs, First Footing is less common than it was even twenty years ago.

Christmas future

As we have seen, many of the Christmas traditions that have come down to us stretch back for thousands of years. Many are specifically Christian, but by no means all. By understanding this rich and fascinating inheritance we can get much more out of our own celebrations. Christmas does not have to be a time when all we do is overeat, overspend and bore ourselves silly with hours of TV 'Christmas Specials' and reruns of old movies. If Christmas is to remain a special festival, then we not only have to cherish the spirit of Christmas past, but also put in something of ourselves that will live on in the future.

We can keep the true spirit of Christmas alive by creating our own traditions and customs within our family and circle of friends. It may be in small ways, such as adding one Christmas tree ornament every

A poor child waits forlornly for Santa Claus. From an American magazine of 1874.

year, and building up a collection as the years pass. Or it might be by adapting an old tradition such as 'Stir-up Sunday', when all the family work together on one part of the preparation of the Christmas feast.

The best custom of *all*, though, is to reach out to those who are less fortunate. You can create your own Christmas tradition by organizing family and friends to 'adopt' a charity or cause and make some kind of contribution, however small, each Christmas time. This contribution may not even involve money or gifts. Perhaps even more importantly, it will mean that you take some time to make contact with a lonely neighbour, or a friend who is unhappy, or just someone who feels left out. But remember, although 'Christmas comes but once a year', the spirit has to be kept alive all 365 days.

INDEX